SEARS HOMES OF ILLINOIS

Sears Homes of Illinois

Rosemary Thornton

Charleston · London
The History Press

Published by The History Press
Charleston, SC 29403
www.historypress.net

Copyright © 2010 by Rosemary Thornton
All rights reserved

Front cover: From the 1910 Sears Modern Homes catalog.
Back cover: Catalog image and drawings from the 1936 Sears Modern Homes catalog; photos by Rosemary Thornton.
All images are from the author's collection unless otherwise noted.

First published 2010

Manufactured in the United States

ISBN 978.1.59629.939.9

Library of Congress Cataloging-in-Publication Data
Thornton, Rosemary Fuller.
Sears homes of Illinois / Rosemary Thornton.
p. cm.
Includes bibliographical references.
ISBN 978-1-59629-939-9
1. Prefabricated houses--Illinois--History. 2. Architecture, Domestic--Illinois--Pictorial works. 3. Sears, Roebuck and Company. Home Construction Division--History. I. Title.
TH4819.P7T484 2010
643'.2--dc22
2010034172

Notice: The information in this book is true and complete to the best of our knowledge. It is offered without guarantee on the part of the author or The History Press. The author and The History Press disclaim all liability in connection with the use of this book. All rights reserved. No part of this book may be reproduced or transmitted in any form whatsoever without prior written permission from the publisher except in the case of brief quotations embodied in critical articles and reviews.

Contents

Acknowledgements   7

1. The House That Father Built   9
2. Sears Homes and Illinois   21
3. Good, Better or Best   34
4. Pretty Little Houses and Pretty Big Losses   39
5. How to Identify a Sears Home   44
6. Frequently Asked Questions   60
7. Conclusion   71

The Gallery   77
Bibliography   173
About the Author   176

Acknowledgements

In spring 2010, I spent three weeks in Illinois and traveled 2,600 miles researching this book. Along the way, I stayed with many kind souls and enjoyed their company. I am supremely grateful for the many kindnesses they showed me.

First, thanks to Dr. Rebecca L. Hunter, who spent three days driving me around the suburbs of Chicago, showing me a few of the many Sears homes that she'd discovered and catalogued. If I'd had to traverse Chicago on my own, my black-and-white picture would now be prominently featured on the back of a milk carton under the heading, "Have you seen this woman?" Chicago and its suburbs are very confusing to a flatlander tourist like myself. Rebecca also freely shared years of research, providing me with lists of Sears homes she'd found in other cities in Illinois.

Thank you to Dale Patrick Wolicki, who has spent the last ten years sharing what he's learned about Sears homes in particular and kit homes in general. Dale has always been willing to share his catalogs, his time, his discoveries and his knowledge.

My brother Tom and his wife Sue live in southwestern Illinois, and during my visit to the Midwest, they lent me their home, their car and their computer. Without their support, love and prayers, the enormity of this writing project would have surely overwhelmed me.

Thanks to Linda Riggs Morgan and Dennis Riggs for giving me countless hours of their time, for sharing their family's wonderful story and for allowing me to photograph their Sears Osborn from every angle imaginable.

And there's Richard Kearney in Cairo, who spent an entire day with me in March, showing me all the Sears-related sights in southern Illinois. As we drove along bucolic country roads (which didn't even show up on my GPS!), Richard was the perfect tour guide, providing an amazing bit of color about the region and its fascinating history. Thank you, Richard, for opening my eyes to that area's inimitable and amazing past!

Thanks to Joyce St. Michael for giving up a day of her life to accompany me throughout Mattoon, Westfield, Casey, Charleston and surrounding areas. And thanks to

Donna Boatman in central Illinois for being my friend, my confidante and number-one cheerleader and for giving me a quiet place to rest and pray and recharge.

And a big chubby thank-you to my husband, Wayne, for understanding that Sears homes are one of the most important things in my life.

Lastly, in the words of Handel, SDG. It's recorded that Handel wrote "SDG" at the bottom of all of his music. SDG is an abbreviation of the Latin phrase "Soli Deo Gloria," or "To God alone, all glory." Researching and writing book-length manuscripts has always been an extremely challenging task for me. Throughout this project, I prayed frequently and diligently, asking God to teach me and lead me. Whatever good this book imparts and whatever blessings may come are practical proofs of Her infinite love.

Chapter 1
The House That Father Built

On that hot, sticky summer day in August 2002, five people showed up at my book signing in Champaign, Illinois. Five.

Hardly made my three-hour drive from Alton seem worthwhile.

That was, until I met Mrs. Riggs. Accompanied by her daughter, Muriel Riggs had put forth a significant effort to attend my book signing. Sitting in a wheelchair, Mrs. Riggs cradled a crumbly, yellowed set of blueprints in her long, thin arms. A similarly aged catalog rested in her lap. Intrigued by the vintage materials, I walked toward her, knelt down and introduced myself. I asked if I could see the blueprints. She clutched them a little tighter to her chest and said thoughtfully, "I don't know. Let's talk for a minute."

She told me that she'd lived in a Sears house since 1928. When she was in eighth grade, her family home had burned to the ground, and her father ordered their new home from the Sears Roebuck catalog. The twelve thousand pieces of house arrived by boxcar at the local train station. Wagonload by wagonload, the building materials were transported to the family farm, just south of Sidney, Illinois. The house was assembled by her father, Henry Mohr, and his brother-in-law Frank, a carpenter by trade.

Within a few months, the house was complete, and the family settled into their new Sears home. In 1939, Muriel Mohr became Mrs. Muriel Riggs, and after the war, she and her husband moved onto the family farmstead. After her parents passed on in 1975, Mrs. Riggs moved back to her childhood home, the Sears Osborn.

Mrs. Riggs carried with her *the* 1928 Sears Modern Homes catalog, from which her parents had ordered their Osborn. In the 141-page catalog, it was described as a bungalow "from the Golden West."

As she handed me the catalog, it opened effortlessly to the timeworn page that featured their house. Some ciphering in the margins showed there'd been quite a bit of thought as to how many extras they could afford. Could they go with the Hercules Steam Heating Outfit, or would they need to settle for the pipeless furnace?

In the center of the page, where the price would have appeared, there was a jagged hole. I asked Mrs. Riggs about it. "Mama didn't want anyone knowing what we paid for the house," she told me with a sweet smile. "She's the one who carved out the price."

Mrs. Riggs's story made my three-hour trip to Champaign very worthwhile.

Each and every one of the seventy thousand Sears homes that were built in the early years of the twentieth century has a similar "back story." They're stories of sacrifice and hard work and indefatigable effort and persistence and success. They are all stories of the American Dream come to fruition.

Let's back up a bit. You may be wondering, what is a Sears home?

In the early 1900s, you could order just about anything from the Sears Roebuck catalog: plows, obesity powders, electric belts (for impotence), cream separators, chicken coops, sewing machines, cookstoves and complete houses.

In 1895, Sears Roebuck and Company issued its first building materials catalog and began selling lumber, hardware, millwork and other building materials, in addition to the tens of thousands of items already offered in the general merchandise mail-order catalog.

In 1908, a headline appeared on page 594 of the Sears general merchandise catalog that read, "$100 set of building plans free. Let us be your architect without cost to you." Customers were invited to write in and ask for a copy of Sears new *Book of Modern Homes and Building Plans*, which featured house plans and building materials.

The 1928 Sears Modern Homes catalog from which Ethel Mohr tore out the price because she didn't want people to know how much she paid for her house.

The first Modern Homes catalog was issued in 1908 and offered more than forty house designs, ranging in price from $495 to $4,115. In addition to the kit homes, Sears offered plans and building materials for a do-it-yourself kit schoolhouse: price—$11,500

Sears's timing was perfect. In 1900, only 8,000 cars were on America's roads. Eight years later, the Model T was introduced. By 1910, 460,000 automobiles were registered and licensed. People were heading to the suburbs, and Sears had just the house for them.

After receiving the Modern Homes catalog and selecting a design, buyers were asked to send in one dollar, and by return mail, they'd receive a bill of materials and full blueprints. The bill of materials listed the items that would come with their home but didn't include precise quantities. Sears, the marketing genius, knew how to sell the sizzle without giving away the steak.

When the buyer placed the actual order for the home-building materials, the one dollar was credited toward the purchase, and the working blueprints and precise bill of materials would be sent.

A few weeks after the order was placed (and paid for), one boxcar containing about twelve thousand pieces of house would arrive at a nearby train depot. The lock on the boxcar was sealed with wax when shipped from the mill. It was the buyer's responsibility to break the seal, inventory the contents (hope you're a fast counter!) and then unload the boxcar. Typically, the railroads would give the buyer twenty-four to forty-eight hours to unload the boxcar. All those pieces and parts had to be transported

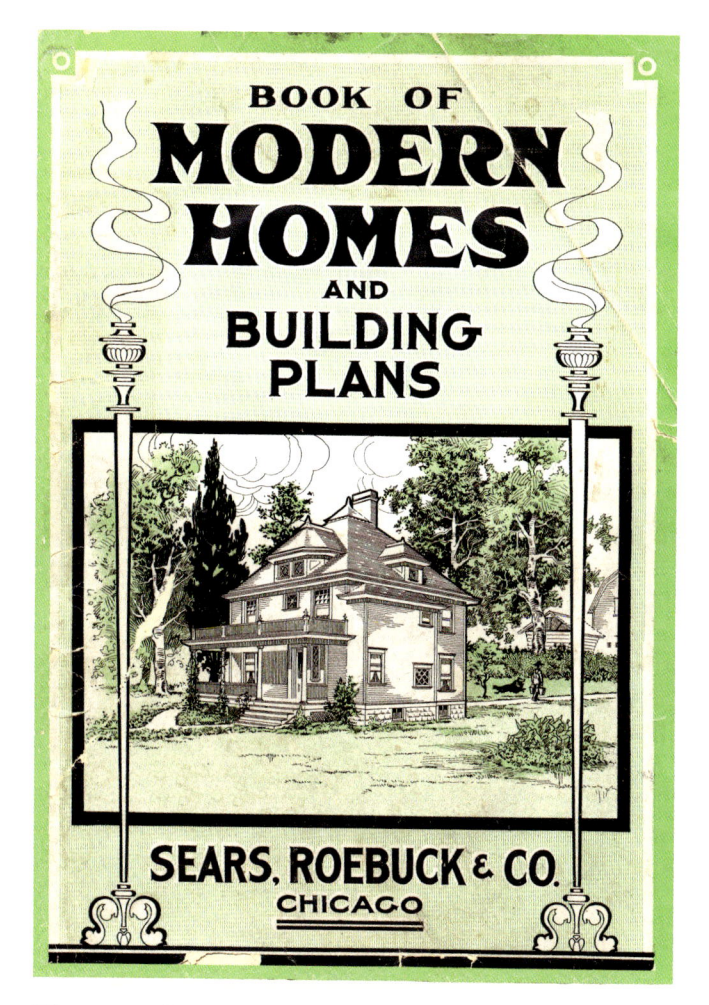

The cover of the first Modern Homes catalog shows a Foursquare with a pyramidal hip roof. However, Sears never offered this particular house at any time in its thirty-two-year history.

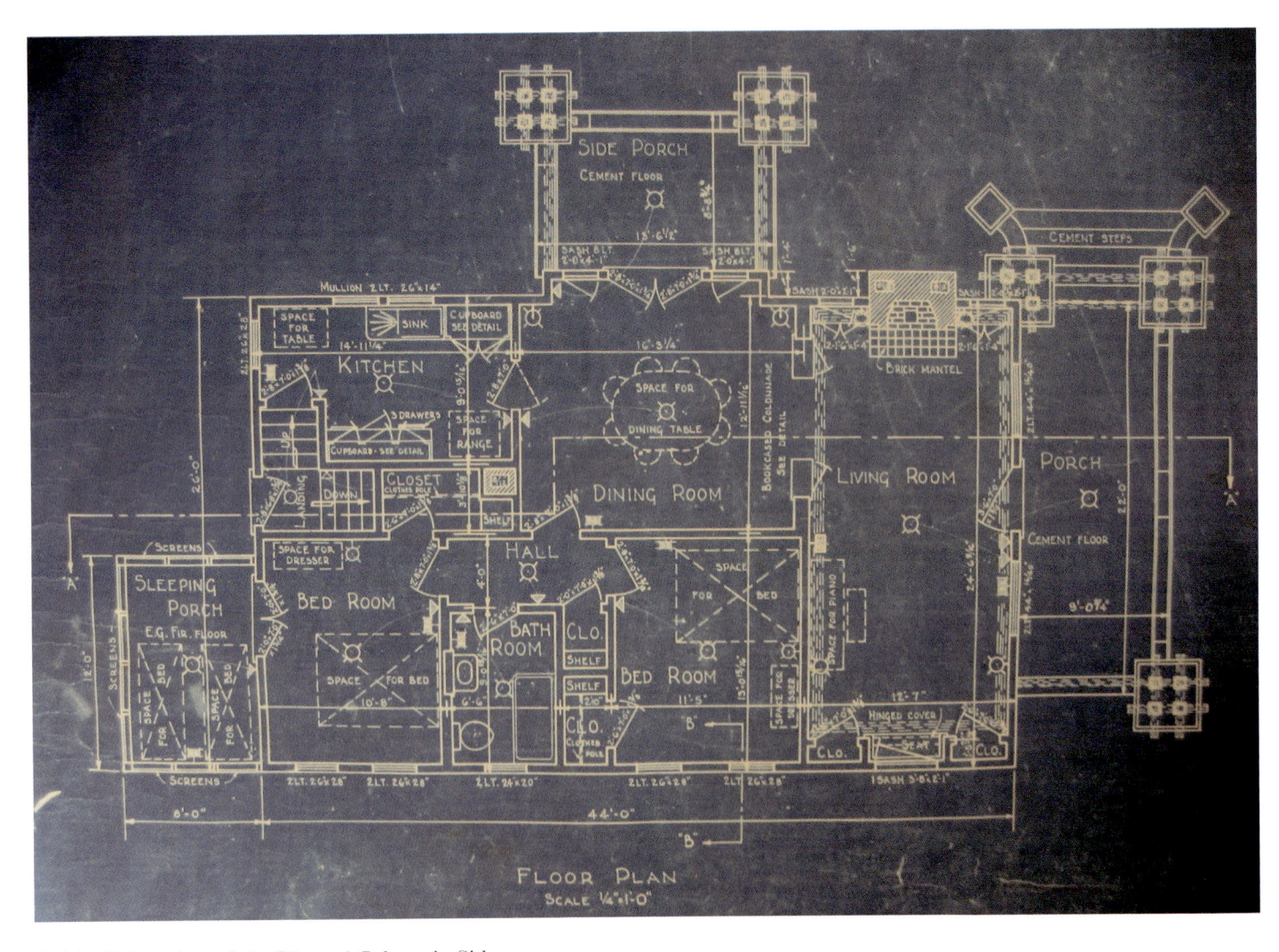

Original blueprints of the Riggses' Osborn in Sidney.

to the building site. (By the way, this is the reason that you'll usually find Sears homes within one to two miles of railroad tracks. It took a lot of trips with a horse and wagon and/or Model T truck to relocate all the contents of one early twentieth-century boxcar!)

If you purchased an "Already-cut and fitted home" (first offered in 1915), the framing members—joists, rafters and studs—were precut and ready to be nailed into place. Each piece of lumber was stamped with a letter and a three-digit number to facilitate construction.

A seventy-five-page leather-bound instruction book, with the homeowner's name embossed in gold on the cover, gave precise directions on the proper placement of those twelve thousand pieces of house. The book offered this somber (and wise) warning: "Do not take anyone's advice as to how this building should be assembled."

Sears estimated that the average man could erect a "Modern Home" in about ninety days, in good weather. That was probably a little on the ambitious side.

A few years ago, a woman called and told me that she and her husband lived in a Sears home that was built in 1947.

"Well, actually, Sears stopped selling kit homes in 1940," I replied.

"Oh you don't understand," she continued. "We bought the kit home in 1939 and *finished* it in 1947."

Aspiring homeowners purchased kit homes hoping to save a little money and create sweat equity. Typically, buyers could expect to save about one-third by building a kit home (compared to traditional stick-built homes).

Some of the more ambitious advertisements claimed that homebuyers would save up to 50 percent by building their own kit homes.

If you could retire from your job and do nothing but work on your kit home, the ninety-day estimate might be realistic, but if you were a working stiff trying to build a house in your spare time, you'd probably need a little more than three months.

About 50 percent of the time, homeowners built these kits on their own. The other half hired a builder or carpenter to put together all those pieces and parts. In 1908, Sears estimated that a carpenter would charge $450 to erect "The Chelsea," a spacious two-story Foursquare with a hipped roof and a shed dormer in the attic. Masonry (block, brick, cement) and plaster were not included in the kit, but the bill of materials advised that 1,300 cement blocks would be needed for the basement walls in the Chelsea.

According to Sears, a painter would want $34.50 to apply the twenty-seven gallons of paint and varnish that came with the house. The plasterer's bill would be about $200.00, which included nailing up 840 square yards of wooden lath and applying three coats of plaster.

Heating equipment, plumbing and electrical fixtures were not part of the package but could be ordered separately from Sears. These houses were shipped to Florida, Wisconsin, California and Virginia, and different locales had different electrical, plumbing and heating needs. Plus, these items were offered at three price levels, giving customers the option to choose "good,

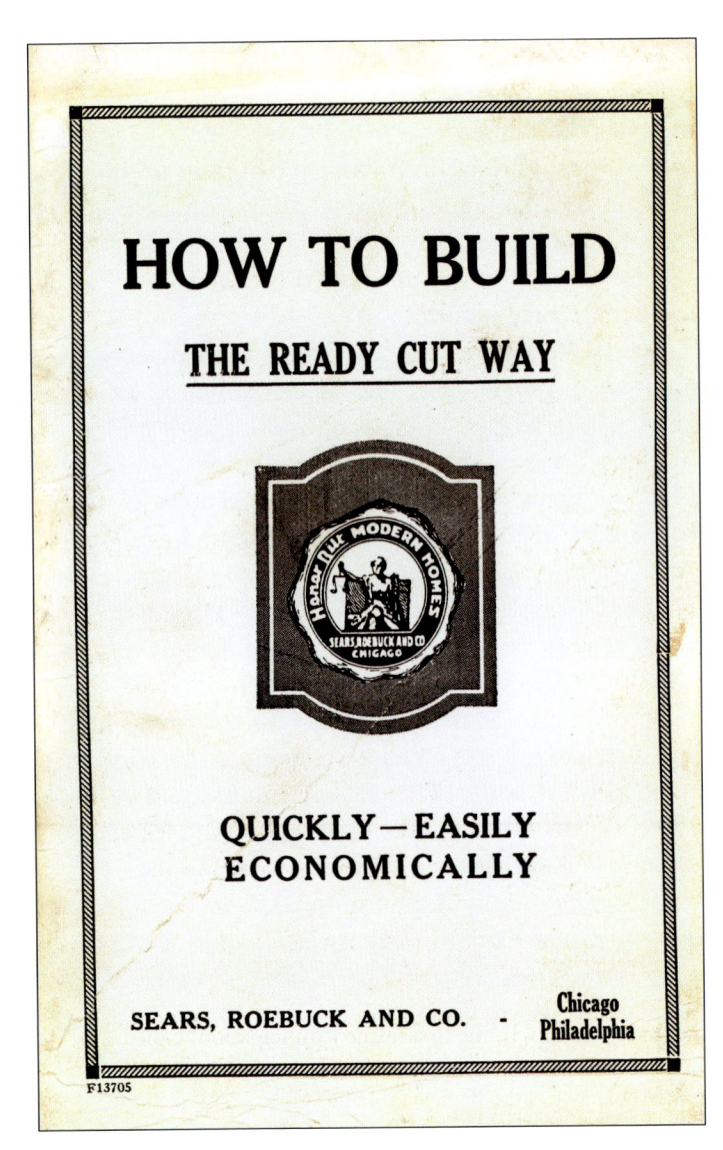

Left: Each Sears kit house came with a seventy-five-page instruction book. In the early years, the instruction book had a leatherette cover with the owner's name inscribed (in gold!) on the cover. These books—together with a detailed set of blueprints—told the aspiring homeowner how to assemble all those pieces and parts of house. These instruction books are very rare. Often, they were discarded after the house was complete.

Below: Many of these instruction books were not specific to the house being built but offered generic information on how to assemble a Sears kit home. The blueprints were specific to the house being built and contained an incredible amount of detail, such as how far apart to space nails.

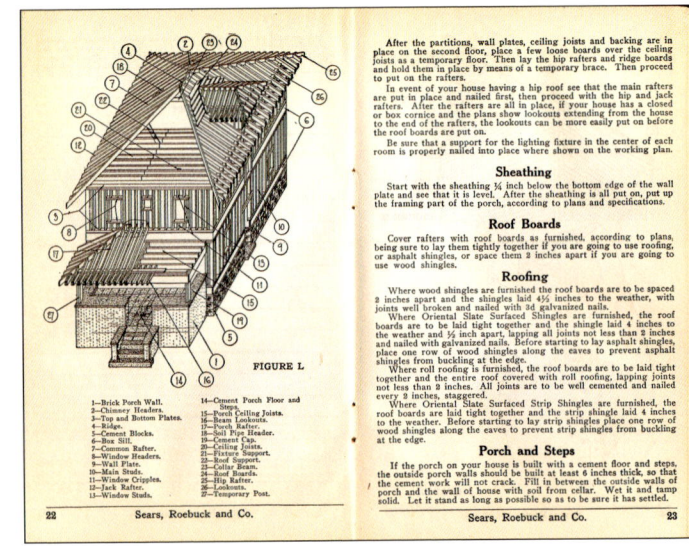

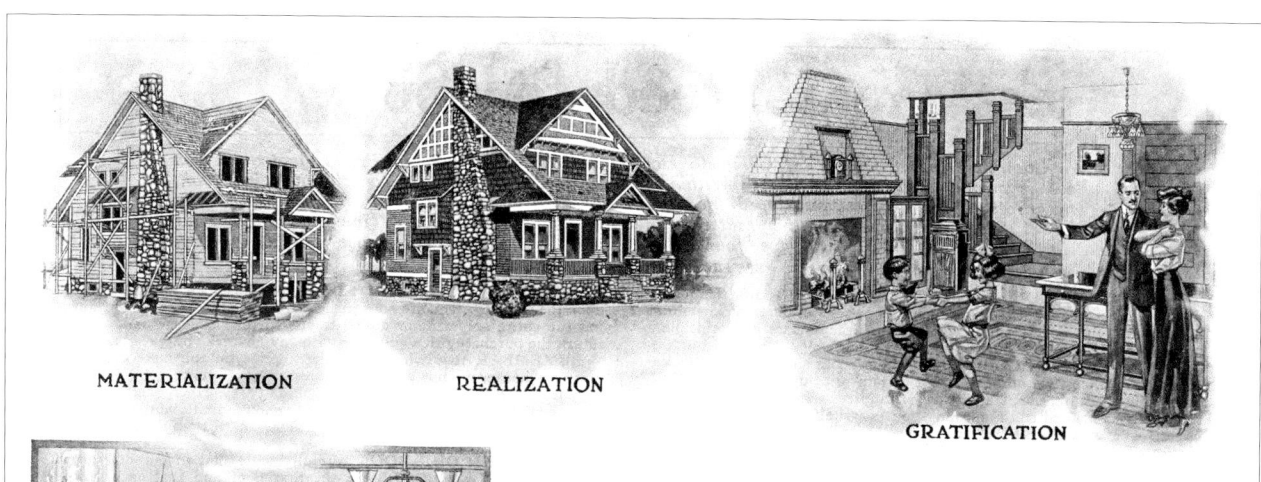

Images in these early catalogs sold Americans on the dream of home ownership. In the first frame ("anticipation"), the family is living in a crummy house with gaslights, sparse furnishings and a sad-looking library table. In the last frame ("gratification"), they now have electric lights, a phonograph, a big fireplace and the library table has grown a marble top, all thanks to Sears!

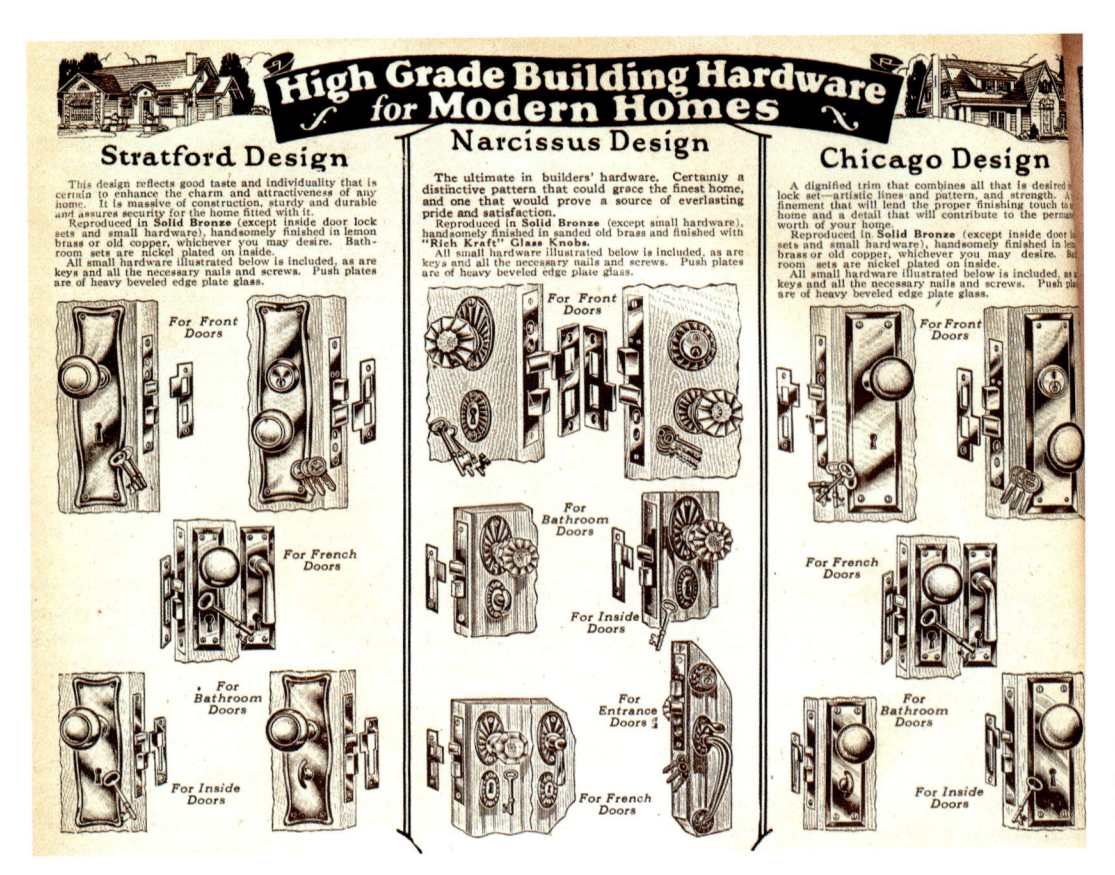

Good, better or best. Sears offered customers three levels of quality (and price) for its kit homes.

better or best" for their home. And sometimes these kit homes were more modern than the communities into which they were sold. Not all communities had municipal water systems and electrical service in the early 1900s. Not much sense in spending money on the Hiawatha Plumbing Outfit if there's no water service available at your site.

When World War I ended in 1918, housing analysts estimated that one to two million homes were needed immediately. The constant flood of immigrants pouring in through Ellis Island also exacerbated the housing shortage.

At a time when skilled labor and quality lumber (both of which were needed to build homes) were in

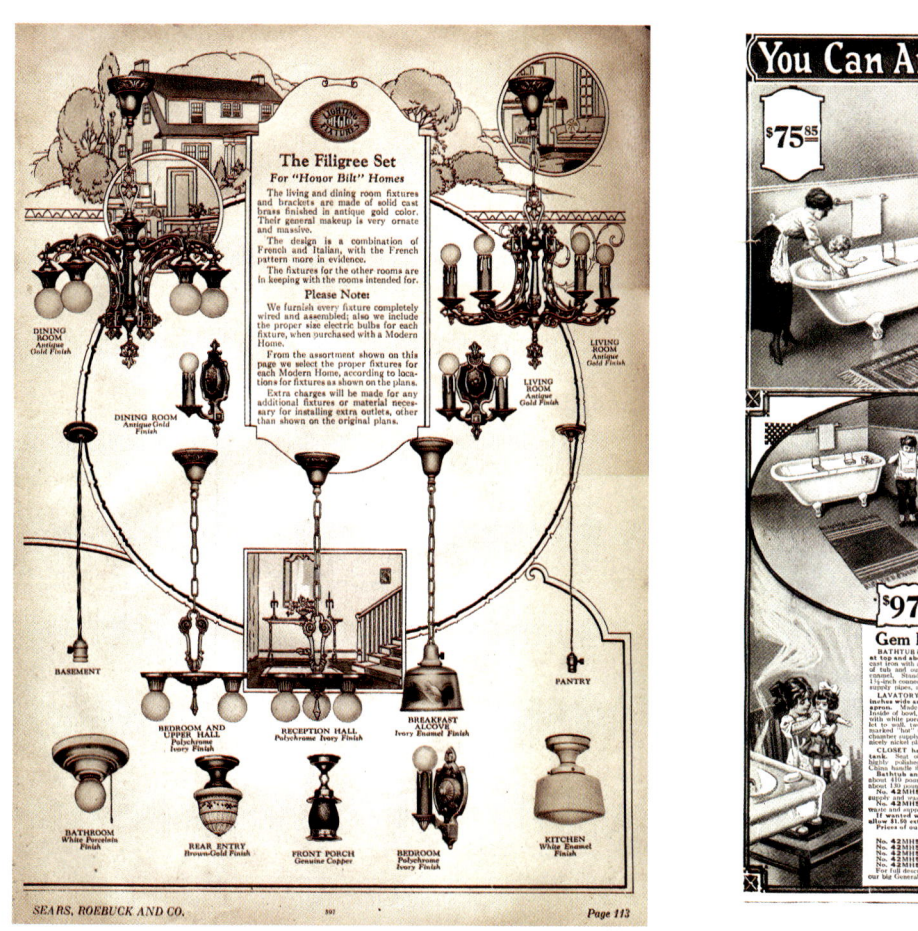

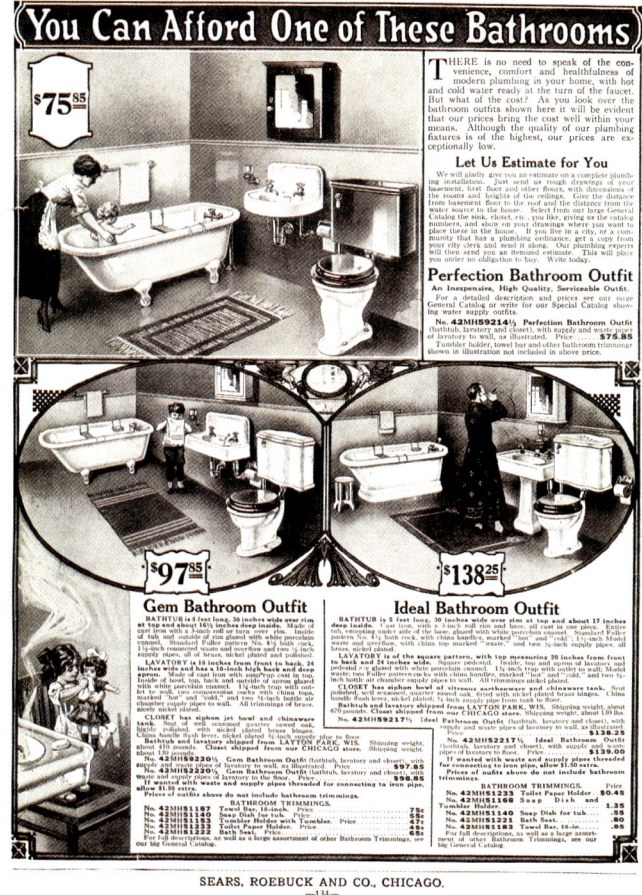

Above, left: The Filigree Light Set provided the perfect finishing touch for your Honor Bilt home.

Above, right: Plumbing, heating and electrical equipment were not included with your kit home but could be purchased separately. Sometimes, these homes were more modern than the communities into which they were sold. Many early twentieth-century building sites did not have municipal water systems and electricity.

short supply, Sears was ready and waiting with its Sears Modern Homes catalog. A kit home, which contained everything you needed to build a house, solved the problem of lumber shortages. Precut lumber obviated the need for skilled carpentry. (That's assuming, of course, that the buyer had an "elementary understanding of construction techniques.")

Sears offered 370 housing designs during its thirty-two years in the kit home business. In addition to traditional bungalows and cottages, it offered Foursquares, Colonial Revivals, Spanish Revivals, neo-Tudors, Cape Cods and more. The Magnolia was Sears's biggest, grandest, fanciest house, with 2,900 square feet, twelve rooms, two and a half bathrooms and two-story Ionic columns spanning the massive front porch. (The Magnolia's style is best described as a Georgian Colonial Revival, but if you look at it closely, it looks a lot like a supersized American Foursquare suffering from delusions of grandeur.)

The sale of Sears Modern Homes skyrocketed in the 1920s. The Sears Modern Homes catalog of 1926 was the largest, with 145 pages and more than eighty house designs (not counting barns, garages, outhouses and chicken coops).

According to *Catalogs and Counters, A History of Sears, Roebuck and Company*, the sales of Sears homes crested in 1929 at $12 million. In 1930, sales dropped to $10.6 million, and in 1931 they hit $8.4 million.

As the economic waves of the Great Depression fanned out further and faster, sales of Sears Modern Homes continued to plummet.

By 1931, Sears had sold fifty-seven thousand of these "Modern Homes" throughout the country. And in 1932, the Sears Modern Homes department began operating at a loss for the first time since 1912. The company's annual report stated that sales of its Modern Homes had dropped 40 percent in one year. For the next few years, there would be stops and starts, but the losses of 1932 marked the beginning of the end.

Two years later, in 1934, Sears's annual report to stockholders stated that sales for 1933 were a meager $3.6 million and that the Modern Homes department had been closed. Also in 1934, Sears liquidated more than $11 million of its home mortgages. At a time when the average Sears house cost well under $3,000 (and mortgages were typically a fraction of that amount), this was a staggering sum. Foreclosing on—and evicting—Sears's best customers from their own homes became a public relations nightmare.

The Sears Modern Homes department was reopened in 1935, but the days of Sears's "Easy Payment" home mortgages were over. In subsequent years, sales of Sears Modern Homes never surpassed $3.5 million. The department was closed once and for all in 1940.

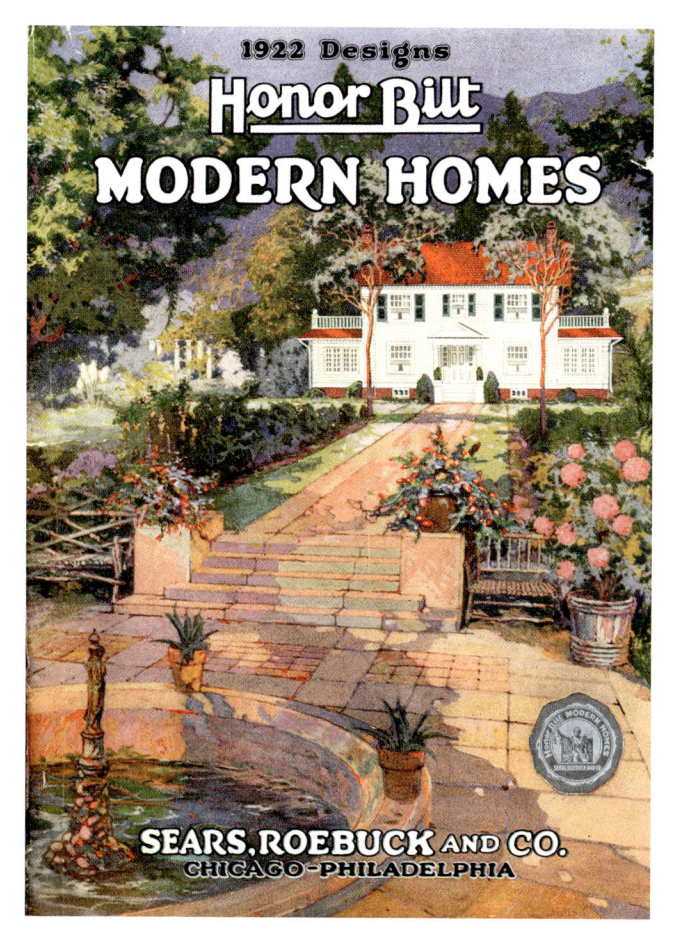

Above, left: "The Hollywood" is the cover girl on the 1921 Sears Modern Homes catalog.

Above, right: In 1922, the Sears Lexington was featured on the cover of the Modern Homes catalog. Note the fishpond in the foreground. These were very popular during this time and were the 1920s equivalent of a triple scoop of your favorite tranquilizer.

The 1940 catalog was a straight reprint of the 1939 Sears Modern Homes catalog. In 1940, Sears closed its Modern Homes department once and for all.

Building a home of your own from a kit was a massive undertaking, but it was a project that thousands of Illinois residents undertook. For several years, I lived in Illinois and traveled throughout the state, looking for Sears homes along the way.

I've found my little pretties sitting majestically in the center of a one-thousand-acre cornfield, and I've found them sitting neatly on city lots no more than thirty feet wide. I've seen Sears homes transmogrified into everything from ostentatious funeral homes to simple country stores to sleazy taverns. Perhaps most interestingly, I've consistently found that more than three-fourths of the people living in these homes had no idea what they had until I knocked on their door and told them. And that's one of the reasons for this book: to help others rediscover this piece of America's almost-forgotten history.

From 1908 to 1940, about seventy thousand homeowners purchased their homes from the pages of the Sears Roebuck catalog. How many Sears homes are in Illinois? Sadly, no one knows. During a corporate house cleaning at Sears, all sales records were destroyed.

However, I do know that Illinois is heavy laden with Sears homes. With few exceptions, I've found at least one Sears home in most of the cities and villages within Illinois. Today, these dandy little houses are just waiting to be rediscovered again so that they can be cherished and valued for what they are: a living monument to a uniquely American piece of our architectural and cultural heritage.

Come sit with me, and let me tell you about the treasures that I've discovered in this great state of Illinois.

Chapter 2
Sears Homes and Illinois

The enchanting story of Sears homes has one common theme woven throughout its history: Illinois.

CHICAGO: Sears was based in Chicago for 105 years. In 1887, when Richard Warren Sears's watch company was one year old, he moved it from Minneapolis to Chicago. From 1887 to 1992, Sears's corporate headquarters was in Chicago, and in 1992, the company moved to a large modern building in Hoffman Estates, a Chicago suburb.

CAIRO: In the early 1900s, Sears had a forty-acre mill in southern Illinois. Thousands of boxcars of southern yellow pine (fresh from Louisiana and Mississippi) were shipped to Cairo, Illinois, and then milled into ready-to-assemble houses at the enormous facility.

CARLINVILLE, WOOD RIVER AND SCHOPER: The largest order Sears ever received for its homes—a $1 million order—was placed by Standard Oil in 1918. Their $1 million check bought 192 modest two-story homes for refinery workers and miners in Carlinville, Wood River and Schoper, Illinois. Today, 152 of those houses still stand in Carlinville, in a working-class neighborhood called Standard Addition. Another 23 also stand proud on Ninth Street in Wood River, all lined up on the same side of the street, shoulder to shoulder, standing strong against the storms of life, economic downturns and pesky vinyl siding salesmen.

ELGIN: Southwest of Chicago, this suburb has the largest known collection of Sears homes in the country. The town most famous for its watches boasts more than two hundred little pretties within its borders.

NAMING NAMES: Sears homes were named after cities in the Midwest, with a preponderance of names coming from Illinois cities and villages. (Houses were first given names in the 1918 Sears Modern Homes Catalog. Prior to this, those dandy little Bungalows and Foursquares and Colonials were known only as Modern Home #106 or, my personal favorite, Modern Home #264P202.)

In fact, 107 Sears homes were named after places in Illinois. And while there's a Magnolia, Illinois, there are no Magnolias in Illinois. Sears Magnolias, that is. Years ago, I grabbed my favorite purple marker and a map of Illinois and endeavored to mark a spot on every city for which a Sears house had been named.

From Adeline to Kilbourne to Palmyra to Yates, I marked them all. It was my fondest hope that when I was done, my pattern of purple marks would reveal a hidden message. At the very least, I was hoping my 107 dots would form the shape of a state-long "S" (for Sears). No such pattern could be discerned. Disheartened and discouraged, I put down the purple marker and went to bed. Lying awake in the dark, I thought about taking the first letter of each city name from north to south and seeing if *that* spelled out "I buried Paul" or some other clandestine message.

A Little History about Sears and Its Presence in Chicago

In 1886, Richard Warren Sears was working in Redwood Falls, Minnesota, as a railway station agent. A shipment of watches arrived at the train station and was refused by the local merchant. Sears contacted the supplier and offered him $50 for the unwanted watches. Selling the watches to other railway agents and passengers, Sears turned $50 worth of watches into $500 in a few months.

A few months later, twenty-three-year-old Sears invested his $500 cash profit into a new watch business and called it the R.W. Sears Watch Company. He advertised his watches in regional newspapers, and in 1887, he moved from Minneapolis to Chicago.

The same year, Sears hired a young watch repairman from Hammond, Indiana. The young man's name was Alvah Curtis Roebuck. Richard Sears and Alvah Roebuck became good friends and eventually became partners in the business venture that they named Sears Roebuck and Company.

Four years later, Sears and Roebuck published their first mail-order catalog, offering jewelry and watches within its 52 pages. By 1893, the little watch and jewelry catalog had grown to 196 pages and offered a variety of items, including sewing machines, shoes, saddles and more. One year later, another 300 pages were added, creating a 507-page mail-order catalog.

In 1895, Alvah Roebuck decided he wanted out. The thirty-one-year-old watch repairman felt that the business was growing too fast and the enormous burden of debt, combined with Sears's wild ways of doing business, were too much for mild-mannered, methodical Alvah. He asked Sears to buy his one-third interest in the company for $25,000.

Of course, Sears didn't have that kind of cash on hand, so he offered Chicago businessmen Aaron Nusbaum and Julius Rosenwald (Nusbaum's brother-in-law) a one-half interest in the company. The price was $75,000, or $37,500 each. Six years later, in 1901, Rosenwald and Sears bought Nusbaum out and paid him $1.25 million for his share of the business.

Following a nationwide depression in 1907, Rosenwald and Sears were at loggerheads on the best course of action to weather the economic storm. This disagreement seemed to highlight their radically different methods of doing business.

On November 1, 1908, forty-four-year-old Richard W. Sears emerged from a terse closed-door meeting with Rosenwald and announced that he would resign as president from his own company. Sears's reason for retiring: he "didn't see the work as fun anymore." A short time later, Sears sold his stock for $10 million. There was another reason for his departure. Sears wanted more time to take care of his ailing wife, who had suffered from ill health for years.

In September 1914, at the age of fifty, Sears died, having turned $50 worth of pocket watches into a multimillion-dollar mail-order empire. His estate was valued at more than $20 million.

Ten years later, Chicago radio station WLS signed on the air, a promotional arm for Sears. The radio station's call letters stood for "World's Largest Store." In 1925, Sears's first retail store opened in Chicago. In 1945, annual sales at Sears Roebuck (retail stores and catalog sales) surpassed the $1 billion mark.

THE SEARS MILL IN CAIRO, ILLINOIS

Cairo's location at the confluence of the Ohio and Mississippi Rivers made it a natural for shipping and distribution. At the turn of the last century, four major rail lines went through Cairo (pronounced "Care-oh"), enabling it to become a centralized

The first issue of Sears's employee newsletter. *WLS* (also the name of its Chicago radio station) stood for "World's Largest Store." This first newsletter featured a story about a happy family that purchased and built a Sears Modern Home.

shipping point for lumber harvested from the South and sent to the North.

In November 1911, Sears announced the opening of the Cairo mill with a two-page advertisement in *American Carpenter and Builder Magazine*. It was headlined "Great News for Builders":

> *Shipments have begun from our second and newest great lumber plant in Illinois. We can deliver you bright, fresh, clean lumber at manufacturer's prices almost as quickly as you can haul makeshift sizes and weatherworn stock from a high priced neighboring lumber yard. Our millwork is sheltered from rain, sun, soot and wind. Our new Illinois plant is located on two of the largest and fastest railroads in the North with direct connections to over 20 different railroads.*

Weatherworn stock was a reference to the fact that, unlike Sears, many mills did not keep their lumber under roof.

Another advertisement in *American Carpenter and Builder* in February 1912 featured a line drawing of the Cairo mill—showing a power plant, six huge warehouses, planing mills, steam dry kilns, log train ramps and log ponds. The mill produced everything for the Ready-Cut (precut) Sears homes except millwork. Sears's mill in Norwood, Ohio, supplied most of the millwork, such as windows, doors and interior trim and moldings.

The plant manager at the Cairo mill was Fred K. Wheeler. After he left Cairo, he wrote a delightful

This image from the 1916 catalog hints at the enormity of the forty-acre mill in Cairo, twenty acres of which were "under roof."

manuscript detailing day-to-day life at the mill. In *Recollection of 36 Years With a Fascinating Lumber Plant*, Wheeler writes that in the early 1920s, 125 houses per month were shipped from the Cairo mill. By 1929, that number had doubled to 250. He relates that in May 1926, a record 324 Ready-Cut houses were shipped. This number did not include the Simplex Sectional (prefab) homes—only Ready-Cut homes.

Houses were shipped from the Cairo mill by land and sea. According to former employees, a few houses were placed on barges and sent on their way via the Mississippi.

Another view of the Sears lumberyard in Cairo, Illinois.

Houses that were sold to nearby locales were shipped by truck. Most went by rail.

By the early 1930s, sales of Ready-Cut homes had dropped precipitously. The mill took on a new line of work: building crates for tractors and other large equipment, including Frigidaire refrigerators and appliances sold by Sears. In the late '30s, the mill produced prefabricated buildings for the camps that housed workers in the Civilian Conservation Corps. Wheeler relates that a typical CCC camp (which included several different buildings) required 400,000 feet of lumber, and about thirty-five of these camps were milled and shipped by the Cairo plant.

In 1940, Sears closed the plant and sold it to the employees. Shortly after the employees purchased the plant, they obtained a contract to build crates for shipping B-17s and other large aircraft overseas for the war effort.

After World War II ended, the former Sears mill—now called Illinois Lumber Company—drafted and published its own book of house plans and tried to sell kit houses again, but without success. The *Cairo Evening Citizen* relates that the plant was liquidated and closed in November 1955.

There are only a few remnants of the old mill in Cairo. There's a bit of a retaining wall on one side of the street, and there's a piece of a cement stoop on the other side. The most substantial reminders of that once-thriving mill are the two Sears Rodessas that sit side by side, a memory of the 1921 experiment that proved the superiority of Ready-Cut Sears Honor Bilt homes over traditional stick-built houses.

Even today, the site of the forty-acre mill is not hard to find if you know where to look. As you head north on Route 37, turn left onto Sears Road and continue until you can't go any farther, and then go a little more. The mill was at the end of that road. Before the interstate highway came through in the 1970s, this street was named the Sears and Roebuck Road. When Sears and Roebuck Road was sliced into two pieces by the highway, the western end became Roebuck Road and the eastern end became Sears Road.

Above, left: The site of the old Sears mill in Cairo, Illinois. The forty-acre parcel is now a farm.

Above, right: At the old Sears mill in Cairo, you can still find this old porch stoop hidden under a tall stack of weeds and overgrowth.

Left: In the early 1900s, the Sears mill was located on Sears and Roebuck Road. In the 1970s when the interstate highway came through, the road was split into two streets, Sears Road and Roebuck Road. Here's the Roebuck side, with a pretty little Sears Wexford in the background.

Far left: Close-up of Roebuck Road sign.

Left: Sears Road. One of the last remnants of the forty-acre Sears Mill in Cairo is the "Sears Road" street sign. Originally, this street was named "Sears and Roebuck Road," but when the interstate came through in the 1970s, it was renamed "Sears Road."

Below, left: Better view of the Wexford on Roebuck Road (near the old mill).

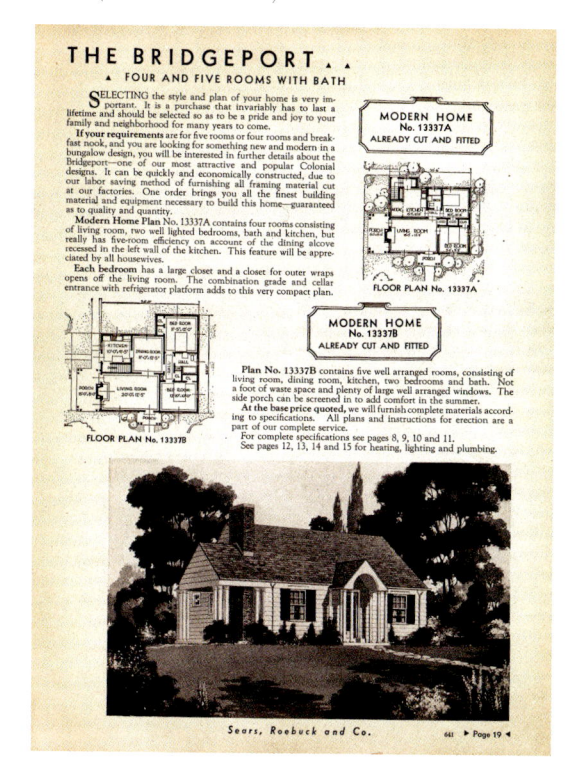

Sears Modern Homes (offered from 1908 to 1940) were true kit homes; they were not prefabricated houses. But after World War II, Sears started selling prefabricated homes and called them Homart Homes. Sectional wall panels were shipped by truck, and the little houses were bolted together at the site. They were very modest, small and economical.

Married by commerce. Divorced by the interstate.

On the Roebuck side of the old Sears and Roebuck Road, you'll find the prettiest little Sears Wexford that you ever did see. At the Sears end, you'll find a pair of Homart Homes, which are *not* the prettiest little houses you ever did see. From about 1947 to 1952, Sears issued a thin twenty-four- to twenty-six-page catalog of ten to twelve prefab houses. These houses were extremely modest and simple, averaging seven hundred to one thousand square feet. They were boxy little houses with the same covered stoop and the same basic floor plan and a low roofline. Prices were not listed in the catalogs, but there was a coupon on the back page for requesting a price quotation. Even by 1950s standards, these were very "economical" homes

Homart Homes were very simple and modest. The house shown on this cover of this 1951 Homart Homes catalog was its most elegant offering. The fireplace and masonry were not included but could be added.

and were true prefab houses (shipped in sections and bolted together at the site). Most of these Homart Homes have not fared well through the decades.

Carlinville, Schoper and Wood River

In 1918, Standard Oil of Indiana made mail-order history when it placed a $1 million order with Sears Roebuck & Company for 192 Honor Bilt homes. It was said to be the largest order in the history of the Sears Modern Homes department. Standard Oil purchased the houses for its workers in Carlinville, Wood River and Schoper in southwestern Illinois. Of those 192 houses, 156 went to Carlinville, 12 were built in Schoper (both sites of coal mines) and 24 were sent to Wood River (site of the refinery). Throughout the 1920s, pictures of these homes were prominently featured in the front pages of the Sears Modern Homes catalogs.

Standard Oil needed great quantities of coal to fire the stills that would convert crude oil into gasoline. Because of shortages in labor and materials brought on by the war, coal supplies were capricious and expensive. News of coal shortages was a recurring headline, and Standard Oil wanted a steady, massive and reliable supply of coal to ensure the continuous operation of its refineries. Carlinville was an especially attractive location because it

A vintage picture of Carlinville's Standard Addition, from the front pages of the 1919 Sears Modern Homes catalog. Note the wooden scaffolding set up around the houses in the foreground.

was on the Chicago and Alton Railroad line and centrally located between Standard Oil's refineries in Whiting, Indiana (near Chicago), and Wood River, Illinois (near St. Louis).

An article in the *Illinois State Journal* on March 27, 1967, entitled "Dear Sirs: Please Send Me 156 Houses" states that a rail line spur—leading directly into Carlinville's newest neighborhood—was built to expedite the unloading the of construction materials from the hundreds of boxcars. Children as young as twelve years old were hired to unload the boxcars full of house parts. They worked ten hours a day and were paid $1.50 for the day's work. It also records that the basements for the Carlinville homes were dug with slip-shovels and horse-drawn scoops. Contractors were paid $17.00 to dig out a basement for the five-room (two-bedroom) houses and $20.00 for the six-room (three-bedroom) houses.

A woman named Mrs. Spaulding supervised the massive building project. "The Lady on Horseback," as she was called, would ride her horse from house to house and keep a close eye on the workmen. She kept the

In 1925, the rear cover of the Sears Modern Homes catalog featured a "certificate of guarantee" and happy testimonial letters from Standard Oil and a customer in Louisa, Kentucky (proud owner of a delightful little Elsmore).

construction workers on their toes. Men she had hired in the early morning were sometimes fired by noon.

The mine at Schoper (located within a tiny town called Standard City) didn't last long or fare well. The houses were built in 1919, and by 1924, the mine started shutting down for longer and longer periods of time, and financial setbacks hit Schoper extra hard.

And what became of those twelve Sears homes across from the mine? According to longtime residents, most of the Sears homes left the same way they came in: in pieces and loaded on a boxcar. A few years after Schoper mine closed, nine of the Sears houses were disassembled and shipped by train to destinations unknown. Two of the Sears houses were moved, intact. They didn't get too far from their original site; one was moved to Route 108, and another house was moved to Atwater Road, both of which are just outside Standard City.

The Gladstone, the last survivor of its eleven siblings, became rental property after its owners passed on. In the mid-1990s, it caught fire and burned to the ground.

In summer 2002, the Schoper powerhouse—the last structural remnant of the Standard Oil Coal Mine—was finally demolished. According to the *Macoupin County Enquirer*, the 213-foot-tall smokestack was brought down August 27 at 10:19 a.m. with carefully placed explosives.

Standard Oil Company of Indiana opened a refinery in Wood River (about thirty miles from Carlinville and across the Mississippi River from St. Louis) in January 1908. The refinery was an enormous operation. By 1919, the *Stanolind Record* reported that the refinery covered 630

The twenty-three Sears homes on Ninth Street in Wood River.

sandy acres and contained 207 stills and could process sixteen thousand barrels of crude each day. Standard Oil recruited and hired hundreds of workers to fill the expanding workforce. But housing in Wood River was woefully inadequate.

In 1920, the census showed that the population of Wood River had increased more than 4000 percent (to 3,476), making it the fastest growing city in the *country* and earning it a place in national headlines. In December 1920, *American Carpenter and Builder Magazine* dubbed Wood River "The Miracle City."

Decades later, in the 1970s, Wood River's industrial landscape was changing. Standard Oil, turned American Oil, turned Amoco, was shutting down its refinery in Wood River a little bit at a time. By the mid-1990s, BP Amoco (now BP) had completely pulled out of Wood River, leaving behind some old buildings, a few tank farms and two dozen Sears homes.

As of this writing, the Sears homes in Wood River sell for $50,000 to $90,000. A home that's been extensively remodeled and modernized fetches the higher price. For the most part, the historical significance of these Sears homes—in both Wood River and Carlinville—is not yet appreciated or valued. Decimating, detail-destroying remodeling—that effaces and erases all evidence of the homes' historical significance—continues.

Elgin

In the early 1900s, Elgin was a working-class community with three main rail lines leading to Chicago. About 25 percent of the people who lived in Elgin worked at the Elgin Watch Factory.

When the watch factory left in the 1950s, Elgin sunk into a terrible depression, which turned out to be a blessing in disguise for its two hundred plus Sears homes. In the 1950s and '60s, there was a nationwide trend toward "updating and remodeling" older homes (which included stripping out the features that made these houses historically significant), but because of troubles in the local economy, most of the homes in

Elgin were spared, thus preserving many important architectural features.

Unfortunately, it's not known how Elgin came to be the home of this country's largest known collection of Sears kit homes. Did an Elgin-based industry place an order directly with Sears? Did word of Sears's high-quality building materials spread quickly throughout this small community? One-fourth of the people who worked at the Elgin Watch Factory owned Sears homes. Perhaps they talked amongst themselves on the factory floor as they went about their day's work, inserting little tiny gears and little tiny springs into Elgin watches.

Thanks to the indefatigable efforts of architectural historian Dr. Rebecca Hunter, 213 Sears homes have been identified in Elgin. To learn more about the largest known collection of Sears homes in the country, visit the Gail Borden Public Library in Elgin, and check out *The Elgin Illinois Sears House Research Project* (by Rebecca Hunter). It's a comprehensive photograph-laden manuscript that tells more about Elgin, its history and its Sears homes. This book is also available for interlibrary loan within the state of Illinois. You can also visit Dr. Hunter's website at www.kithouse.org.

Chapter 3
Good, Better or Best

As any long-term Sears patron knows, the company has always offered its product lines in three grades: good, better and best. This was true for its kit homes, too. In the early 1920s, there were three levels of quality: Honor Bilt, Standard Built (also known as Econo-Built) and Simplex Section Cottages.

Honor Bilt homes were the crème de la crème of kit homes and were made with first-class lumber and millwork and utilized traditional construction standards, such as double headers over the doors and windows, double floors (primary floors over subfloors), exterior sheathing under clapboard or cedar shingles and wall studs on sixteen-inch centers. The lesser grades (Standard Built and Econo-Built) had wall studs on twenty-four-inch centers, single headers, no subfloor and no underlying exterior sheathing. They were pretty basic housing.

For a short time in the early 1920s, there was also an ultra-cheap line known as "Lighter Built." Lighter Built was what we'd describe today as a hunting shack, best suited for areas with warm weather, calm winds and serene wildlife. One belligerent moose could relocate your Lighter Built cabin with a minimum of effort.

Simplex Sectional Cottages were at the bottom rung of the construction ladder. These were prefabricated vacation cottages that could be disassembled and packed away when it was time to head home. They were a little better than a canvas tent but were truly very primitive by today's standards.

The 1922 Modern Homes catalog described Simplex Sectional Cottages as "ideal seashore, lake, winter resort houses and substantial garages." The 1919 catalog said that they were ideal for summer or winter resorts because "they can be quickly put up at the beginning of the season and then taken down and moved to a new location."

Walls and gables on Simplex Sectionals came in whole sections, with windows and doors pre-hung in their frames. The small homes could be put together with basic tools, and their assembly required no sawing or nailing. The houses were held together by strap irons, screws, metal clips and bolts. The 1923 catalog promised that two men could assemble the house in eight hours.

The Honor Bilt homes were far and away the best sellers. Probably 99 percent of the houses I've identified in Illinois are Honor Bilt.

In 1916, the terms "Honor Bilt" appeared on the cover of the Modern Homes catalog.

The "already cut and fitted" (precut) lumber (only offered in the Honor Bilt line) offered many benefits to the homeowner but was equally advantageous for Sears. *Catalogs and Counters* states that precutting the lumber lowered shipping charges for Sears, since wastage was removed before shipping. Secondly, Sears could now buy lumber in economical lengths, resulting in additional savings. And, perhaps best of all, Sears could cut the knots out of second-grade lumber and turn it into first-grade stock. The leftover lengths of lumber would be utilized *somewhere* amidst those twelve thousand pieces.

Stumbling about with my flashlight in the dimly lit basements of countless Honor Bilt homes throughout the country, I'm always dazzled by the *quality* of the lumber. Sears's lumber was first-growth lumber. ("First-growth lumber" is the name given to wood that grew slowly in natural forests. The more slowly the wood grows, the denser its grain. Dense wood is strong wood, which is naturally more resistant to decay and rot.)

In *American Carpenter and Builder Magazine* (August 1913), Sears had a two-page advertisement with this pitch: "Any shrewd lumber buyer can easily understand why we are in a position to undersell anyone else on lumber and millwork. We buy raw lumber direct from the greatest timber tracts in America. Second, our mills are located right in the heart of the yellow pine districts."

The yellow pine framing members that support these old Sears homes, now nearing the century mark, are probably harder and denser than most of today's so-called hardwoods. Some of these houses have had only minimal maintenance, yet all these years later, they're still as square and true and solid as the day they were built.

Sears earned a well-deserved reputation for providing the best quality lumber for both framing and millwork, and it was proud of its reputation. In the 1922 Sears Modern Homes catalog under the heading "Important," Sears stated: "We do not handle hemlock, spruce or inferior types of lumber. The lumber we furnish is fine, dry yellow pine, the strongest lumber for framing. Cypress for outside finish, the wood that lasts for centuries; oak, birch or yellow pine, as specified for interior finish."

These kit homes were also offered in brick. Any Sears home could be built with a masonry exterior, such as block, brick or stone. However, because of the shipping costs, Sears suggested that masonry should be obtained locally.

Wooden sidings were the most popular choice for kit homes. The buyer could choose exterior sidings of red cedar, redwood or cypress. Most frequently, exterior sidings were cypress and exterior trim pieces (corner boards, door and window trim, eaves, etc.) were also cypress.

In the late 1920s, Sears published a sales brochure promoting cypress lumber. The title was "Outside finish and trim of Honor Bilt homes made of cypress. The wood that lasts thru the ages." The brochure went on to say:

> *The history of cypress, the wood eternal, runs back through the ages—back to the days of Noah's ark. Cypress was the wood most used among the ancient nations of the world. They made use of cypress for*

practically everything for which wood was needed—musical instruments, furniture, wine presses, boats and ships, palaces and temples. The ancients engraved their laws on cypress boards, carved images of their gods out of cypress logs, buried their kings and queens in mummy cases made of cypress.

The lasting quality of cypress is conclusively proven in the old Louisiana home of Joseph Jefferson, built of cypress almost 100 years ago and still well preserved. Honor Bilt homes have only honest materials in them; materials that we know to be the highest grade that is possible to put into a home. That is why we use cypress, the wood eternal, *to protect all parts exposed to weather.*

(I have two questions. Who is Joseph Jefferson, and what does *dishonest* lumber look like?)

Interior floors on average-priced Sears homes were typically oak on the first floor; maple in the kitchen and bath; and yellow pine on the second floor. In less expensive homes, yellow pine was standard throughout the house for trim moldings, floors and doors. However, you could always upgrade.

The Osborn was a mid-range Honor Bilt home. Through the 1920s, it was offered for $2,700, plus or minus a few hundred dollars. It was described as a California bungalow and was a fine-looking home with many nice features. Maple floors for the kitchen and bath were standard; the other rooms had oak floors. For an additional $148, you could upgrade to oak trim for the

Masonry, wood or stone exteriors were available for your Sears kit home. If you opted for masonry, those materials were obtained locally due to shipping expense.

living room and dining room. An extra $15 bought you a ceramic tile bathroom floor, laid in cement of course, instead of a maple floor.

In the 1920s, wooden roofing shingles were the norm, but for fifty-six dollars, you could upgrade to "Oriental Asphalt Shingles," which were guaranteed for seventeen years. As an added bonus, they were fireproof. (This was a big plus because of the prevalence of coal-fired furnaces. It was not uncommon for hot embers to fly out of the chimney, land on the wooden roof and start a house fire.) If you wanted storm doors and windows for your Osborn, you'd need to send in an extra eighty-one dollars; window screens were an additional sixty dollars.

The Bandon: An Interesting Case Study on the Actual Cost of Building a Sears Home in Illinois

During a research trip to Cairo, Illinois, I stumbled across an incredible document in the vertical files at the Cairo Public Library. It was a handwritten account, apparently written by the original owner, that delineated the cost of building a Sears Modern Home, the Bandon. The house was built in 1921 in Pulaski, Illinois. According to this document, the lumber for this kit home was shipped from the Sears mill in Cairo (about fifteen miles away).

According to records at the Cairo Public Library, this Sears Cyclone barn was built on the same plot with the Bandon in 1924. It was shipped from the mill in Cairo, and the kit barn cost $943.

Cost of the Bandon	$2,794.00
Plaster (extra)	$133.00
Material to finish attic rooms	$241.00
Complete hot water heating system	$403.66
Wire and light fixtures	$133.66
Labor for carpenter (including masonry work)	$1,600.00
Total	$5,305.32

In 1924, a Sears Cyclone Barn (also shipped from Cairo) was built on the same property. The only detail shown in the paperwork shows that the homeowner paid $943 for the Sears Barn.

Chapter 4
Pretty Little Houses and Pretty Big Losses

Owning a home was everyone's dream at the turn of the century, but financially, that dream was out of reach for many young families. Sears's "homes through mail order" tapped right into the heart of that innate desire for homeownership and concurrently lowered the cost of construction with mass production, while maintaining excellent quality.

The kit home that Sears offered included house plans (blueprints), hardware (door knobs, locks, hinges), millwork (doors, windows, moldings), building materials (paint, putty, rain gutters, nails, roofing) and lumber (framing lumber, flooring, siding).

By 1915, Sears was offering "already-cut and fitted houses," which meant that kits were shipped with all the framing lumber precut and ready to be nailed into place. An advertisement on the back cover of the 1918 Modern Homes catalog went so far as to say that no sawing was needed to build a precut Sears home and that you could "hang your saw on a nail all day." While this was an overstatement, the fact is, precut lumber in kit homes saved the average do-it-yourself homebuilder inestimable hours of measuring and sawing (and the inevitable heartache of mistakes and mis-cut lumber).

To appreciate the value of precut lumber, think back to the early 1900s. Electricity was in its infancy, and in many cities, electricity was turned off each night at 11:00 p.m. for six hours of repairs and maintenance! In 1910, only 10 percent of homes had electricity. By 1930, that number had jumped to 70 percent, according to *Electrifying America: Social Meanings of a New Technology*, by David E. Nye. As late as December 1917, *American Carpenter and Builder Magazine* was still describing electric lights as a *luxury* that a builder should incorporate into a modern city home.

To cut a piece of lumber with a handsaw required time, strength and a degree of expertise (for a good square cut). Electric saws and the heavy-duty wiring to handle the amperage draw were a thing of the future. In fact, the electric handsaw (a portable circular saw) wasn't widely available until 1925. A fascinating news item in the February 1925 *American Carpenter and Builder* heralded the "new invention" with this commentary: "The portable circular saw does the sawing for 15 carpenters."

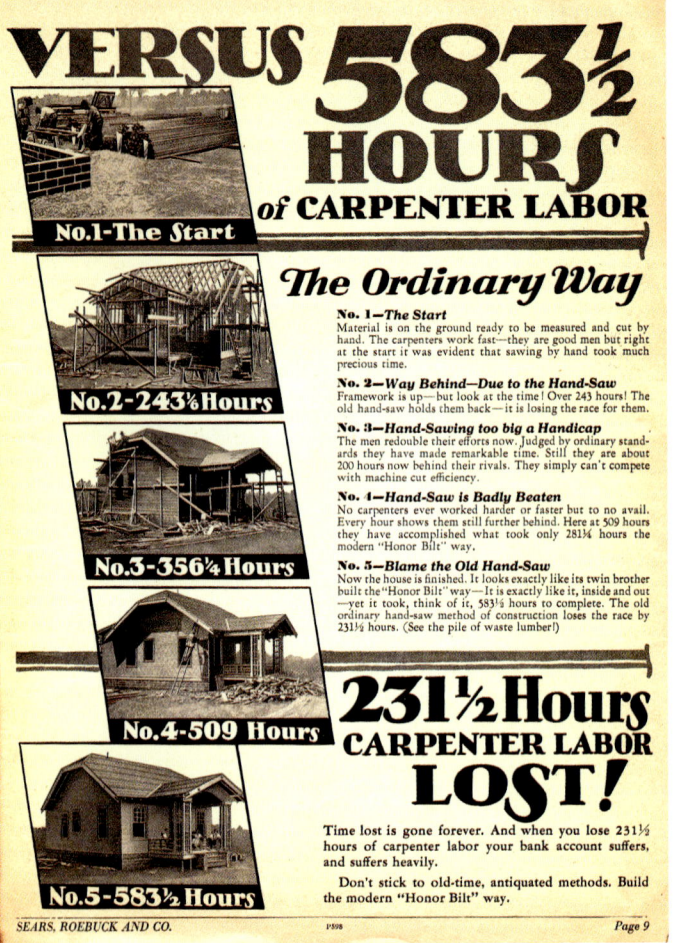

Picture from the 1929 Sears Modern Homes catalog shows "the Experiment," where two Rodessas were built at the Sears Mill. One house was a traditional stick-built home, and the other house was a Ready-cut Sears Modern Home.

In 1921, Sears conducted an "experiment" building two Rodessas (small frame homes) side by side at the site of the Sears mill in Cairo, Illinois. One house was erected using Sears's precut lumber. The second house was built using traditional construction techniques—no precut lumber. The precut house was fully assembled in 352 carpenter hours, and the stick-built home was completed in 583 carpenter hours.

The 1929 Sears Modern Homes catalog featured a blow-by-blow description of the "race" to build the little Rodessas: "Hand saw is badly beaten: No carpenters ever worked harder or faster but to no avail. Every hour shows them further behind. Here at 509 hours they have accomplished what took only 281 hours the modern 'Honor Bilt' way." And further on: "The old ordinary hand-saw method of construction loses the race by 231 hours. See the pile of wasted lumber!"

In 1911, Sears started offering Sears mortgages for its Sears homes, which—through the years—evolved into a delightfully simple loan approval process. A 1920s Sears mortgage application asked a few simple questions about the house and lot but only asked two financial questions: "What is your vocation?" and "How much money can you put into the deal?" If you could answer those two questions satisfactorily, you qualified for a mortgage. (Sears wanted aspiring homeowners to own their lot outright.) Home buying and mortgage qualifying had never been easier.

A "do-it-yourself" modern home must have had a special appeal for a generation that remembered

From the 1929 Modern Homes catalog, this picture demonstrates that obtaining a mortgage from Sears Roebuck is just like having a smiling banker hand you fistfuls of small, unmarked bills. The house shown here is a Willard.

Grandma's soddie on the plains or spent several days at a relative's log cabin in western Illinois. Many midwestern men and women who built Sears kit homes in the early 1900s were raised in housing that would be considered extremely primitive by today's standards. In 1917,

American Carpenter and Builder Magazine reported that "watertight roof, walls and floor are an essential feature of a modern city house." Laura Ingalls Wilder's *Little House* books described very primitive housing on the plains in soddies and tiny cabins in the 1870s, a scant forty years earlier.

The idea behind selling homes through mail order was inspired and brilliant. Sears knew that homeowners both needed and purchased more merchandise than non-homeowners.

One hundred years ago, multigenerational housing was the norm, and young couples often moved in with their parents, who may be living with *their* parents. Boardinghouses were also very common in this time. Sears knew that getting these folks into a home of their own would create new customers and boost sales. By enabling more Americans to become homeowners, he'd be creating a new market for the 100,000 items in his 1,200-page, four-pound mail-order catalog.

Look closely at the floor plans in Sears Modern Homes catalogs and you'll see itty bitty dotted lines showing ideal placement for a graphophone (also known as a phonograph), davenport, piano, library table, beds, dressers and more.

In the late 1920s, Sears hired Miss Mayer, an interior decorator, to figure out the ideal placement for all those itty bitty dotted lines. Part of her job was to ascertain how much furniture could be stuffed inside a four-room

Sears Modern Homes were quite an improvement from the soddies of the plains. These were homes made of rectangular pieces of sod, stacked deep and high.

house with bedrooms that measured eight by nine feet. The marketing scheme was successful, as is evidenced by testimonials like this:

> *I have just recently completed building one of your "Honor Bilt" Modern Homes and want to tell you how well I am satisfied. I saved over $2000 in building this house. You might also like to know that it is furnished with Sears Roebuck rugs, furniture, curtains, wall paper and fixtures. In buying my furniture from you, I saved over half (1929 Sears Modern Homes catalog).*

The 1926 Modern Homes catalog was its largest, with eighty-eight house designs (seventy-three Honor Bilt and fifteen others) offered within its 145 pages. Also in 1926, the Sears mill in Cairo, Illinois (where these homes were milled), shipped out a record-breaking 324 Honor Bilt homes in May, a significant increase from the first years of the 1920s, when it averaged 125 houses per month.

According to *Catalogs and Counters, A History of Sears, Roebuck and Company*, sales of Sears Modern Homes peaked in 1929, at $12 million, with Sears holding more than $6 million in new mortgage loans for these buyers.

And then came the Great Depression. *Catalogs and Counters* says that sales dropped to $10.6 million in 1930, with $6.8 million of that tied up in Sears mortgages. Still, these sales numbers were not too shabby, considering what was happening with the rest of the economy. In January 1931, the *Chicago Tribune* reported that housing starts for the prior year were down 53 percent.

By the end of 1932, the Great Depression had caught up with Sears—with a vengeance. *Fortune Magazine* stated that the sales of Sears homes decreased 40 percent in 1932 and the Modern Homes department had taken a loss of $1.15 million for the year. Two years later, Sears liquidated more than $11 million in mortgages, and the foreclosures were still coming in. It was in 1934 that Sears officially closed the Modern Homes department.

In 1935, the Modern Homes department was reopened, but Sears mortgages were no longer an option. Sales were poor, and the last Modern Homes catalog was issued in 1939. (The 1940 Sears Modern Homes catalog was a reprint of the 1939 edition.) In 1940, the department was closed, and a few years later—during a corporate house cleaning—all the sales records, blueprints and ephemera were destroyed.

Because the sales records were destroyed, the only way to find these Sears homes today is through community surveys, searching street by street and house by house. My friends Rebecca Hunter and Dale Wolicki and I have discovered perhaps twelve to fifteen thousand Sears homes. That leaves at least fifty-five thousand for you to find. Let me tell you how it's done.

Chapter 5
How to Identify a Sears Home

As soon as my lecture on Sears homes came to a close, I saw an elderly woman move through the crowd as she made her way toward the lectern. Walking slowly but purposefully, she held a black-and-white photo in one hand and an aluminum cane in the other.

"I grew up in a Sears home," she told me, her countenance beaming with pride. "My father ordered our house out of the Sears Roebuck catalog, and for the next six months, he spent every spare minute putting it all together. It was a wonderful house."

She set the treasured photo on the lectern's flat surface and gently slid it toward me. I picked up the photo and examined it carefully. It was a classic Foursquare with a hip roof and one small dormer on the third floor. The front porch spanned the entire front of the house.

"This is a lovely home," I told her as graciously as possible, "but it's not a Sears kit home." I handed the photo back to her, smiled broadly and then made eye contact with the next person in line.

She was not so easily dismissed. She put that photo back on the lectern and slid it back to me. In a voice that could best be described as menacing, she growled, "I think you need to take another look."

I did as instructed and then handed the photo back a second time and said, "I'm sorry, but that house does not match any of the 370 designs that Sears offered during its thirty-two years in the kit home business."

The news was not well received. For a moment, I was sure that she was going to smack me with her aluminum cane. Fortunately, she dropped the photo in her purse and toddled off, murmuring things under her breath that can't be repeated in polite company.

This is not an uncommon reaction. About 75 percent of the people who think they live in a Sears home are mistaken. In other words, I am unable to identify their home as being one of the 370 designs that Sears offered during its thirty-two years in the kit home business.

Most often, these "Sears homes" turn out to be kit homes offered by another national kit home company, such as Gordon Van Tine, Aladdin, Montgomery Ward, Sterling, Lewis Manufacturing or Harris Brothers. Or perhaps it came from a regional company (of which

A happy family poses in front of their newly constructed Modern Home #106, circa 1915. Note the detail of the marginal lites on the hipped dormer (and in the original catalog image). It'd be much easier to identify Sears homes if they retained their original appearance.

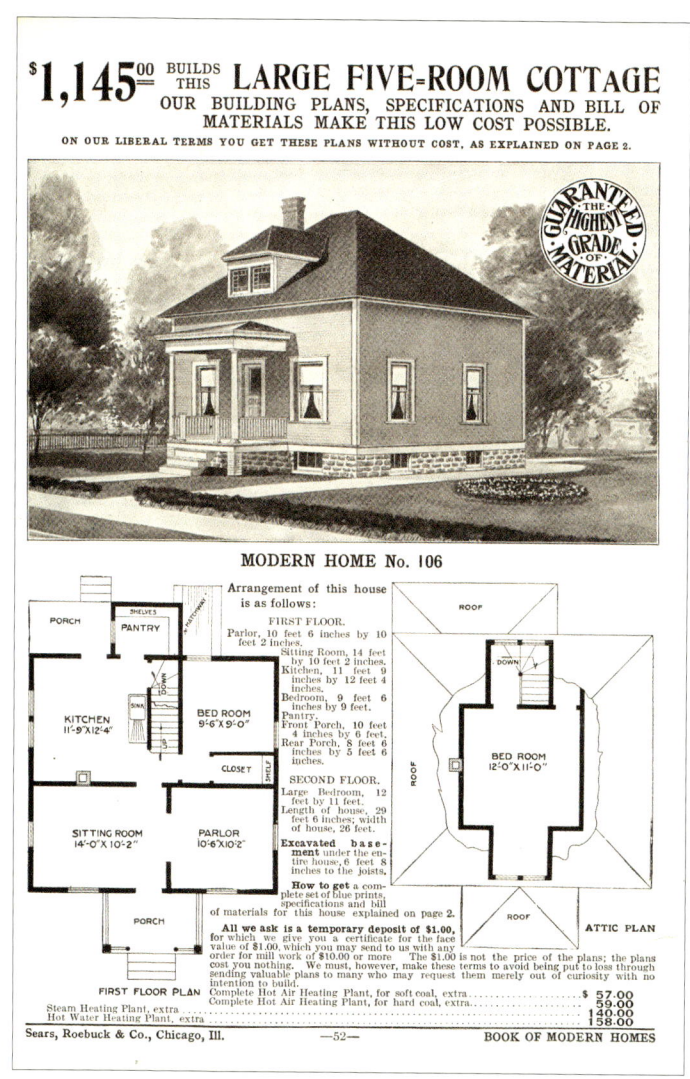

there were *many*). Sometimes, people tell me they've found Sears shipping labels on the back of millwork and moldings, yet the house does not match any of the known designs offered by Sears. In these cases, I suspect that the building supplies for the house were ordered from Sears (which would explain the house "being shipped in boxcars") but with blueprints and building plans from another source. In my opinion, it is not a Sears house unless the design is also from Sears.

One afternoon, I got a call from an elderly couple in a small Illinois town about an hour from my home in Alton. During a windshield survey, I'd identified their home as a possible Sears home, but using my one to ten rating system, I'd given their house a three. In other words, I wasn't very confident that this was the real deal. But then came their frantic phone call, reporting that they'd found marks on the lumber in the basement. I hurriedly jumped into my little red car and made the long drive to their home. After about eighteen seconds of the cursory pleasantries, I pushed them aside and rushed down to their basement. Immediately, I found the "markings" on the lumber. Recently, a newer two-by-eight had been scabbed onto an old rotted joist, and the new lumber bore a blue-ink stamp with the lumberyard's contemporary logo.

I tried not to laugh out loud. It wasn't easy.

During my travels, I met a man who told me about a Sears home his mother had built. "My mother was looking through the Modern Homes catalog," he recalled, "and she couldn't decide between two different houses. She liked the top half [rooflines] of one house and the bottom of another house. She cut these two pictures out of the catalog and taped them together. She sent this taped creation to Sears—with a note asking if they could send her *this* house with *that* roofline—and they said, 'We sure can!'" Imagine trying to identify *that* as a Sears house ninety years later!

Sears architects designed many different houses in many different styles and offered a wide variety of options. Want two dormers instead of one? Want a big dormer or an itty bitty one? Switch from a gable roof to a hip roof? Would you rather have brick in place of clapboard? Take out a window? Add two windows? Reverse the floor plan? Try a different front porch? No problem! Sears encouraged homeowners to customize these houses to suit individual needs.

In the 1930 Sears Modern Homes catalog, under the heading "Complete Architectural Service" is this statement: "If you wish any changes in the design or have any special plan that you would like to have us figure, we can give you the best advice and technical help. Our engineers will be glad to help you build your home as you want it."

A few pages later in the catalog was this: "Prepare a rough outline [of the house you want], showing the approximate size, number of rooms desired and style of exterior preferred. Our staff of architects are at your disposal to prepare these special plans for you."

In the 1930 Sears Modern Homes catalog are photos of two "special" houses. One is a Special Berwyn, which,

Sears assured customers that its Architectural Service would save time, money and headaches, and best of all, Sears customers wouldn't have to pay those architects enormous fees for "untried plans" and the ensuing "risk and disappointment."

according to the caption, has been "increased in size." The other house is a Special Claremont, a modest Neo-Tudor. The caption reads, "Several changes have been made in the above house, which materially increased the cost. The roof was raised and two rooms were added on the second floor."

Sears advertised a variety of upgrades and options throughout its catalogs, such as different entryways, sun porches, second-floor sleeping porches, alternate front porches, side porches and more. While these add-ons could spruce up an otherwise plain-looking home, they also make it incredibly challenging to identify specific models ninety years later.

Modernization and the passage of time create yet another challenge: most of these houses have been altered and remodeled to meet current needs. Many Sears homes were modest and small when originally built. Bedrooms were often eight or nine feet by ten or eleven feet—tiny by today's standards. As housing needs evolved and families needed more space, the houses were changed and expanded.

In the 1930s, substitute-siding salesmen began promising homeowners that their product could put an end to the chore of painting. First came asbestos siding, then asphalt siding, then aluminum and eventually vinyl. Distinctive architectural features were hacked off when substitute siding was installed. Old windows were tossed aside for vinyl replacement windows. Front porches and sleeping porches were enclosed and turned into living space.

Many of the Sears Modern Homes storefronts were quite modest. Here's a picture of one of those storefronts, which was located on the second floor of this building, above the Standard Auto Parts store. Date and location unknown.

Siding salesmen, violent storms, floods, termites, ill-informed remuddlers and people who think wallpaper borders with dancing geese belong in an old house can cause extensive damage to a historical home. (I think of remuddling as "friendly fire." It's a terrible mistake, but the hapless victim still dies.)

Yet Sears homes are just that: *homes*. They are lived in and loved in, and they evolve through the decades. After ninety years, there are inevitably many changes.

Puffed Houses

An elderly man called me at home one night to tell me about a Sears home in southwestern Illinois. He'd lived in the same house for several decades and was certain that the house next door was a Sears home.

"How do you know it's a Sears home?" I asked, hoping for an answer that was credible. The neighborhood he lived in was full of 1950s frame houses. I wondered how there could be a Sears home in *that* area. (Sears homes were sold from 1908 to 1940.)

"It was moved here from another location," he told me, "and I knew the man who built it." The next morning, I drove to the house. It was the Roseberry—a one-and-a-half-story home with one broad, oversized gable dormer.

Staring at this Roseberry, I was puzzled. It was definitely a Roseberry, but it was several feet too wide. An extra-chubby Roseberry. Further investigation revealed it was a *customized* Sears home. A puffed Roseberry.

And Then There Are Mistakes

In *The Comfortable House*, Alan Gowans tells the story of a West Virginia family that purchased a Sears Argyle, a small, attractive and popular Honor Bilt home. The family hired carpenters to build the house, but they put it together *backward*, reversing the floor plan. As soon as the error was discovered, the carpenters were fired and the house was disassembled. This time, the family did their own carpentry, while closely studying that seventy-five-page instruction book. When the house was nearly finished, they realized they'd mixed up the living room and dining room windows. Their Argyle, Gowans relates, still has those two transposed windows on the front of the house.

As mentioned in the prior chapter, when the Sears Modern Homes department closed in 1940, the sales records and promotional materials were destroyed. Now, it's up to individuals and homeowners to seek out and find the Sears homes in their communities. Just remember, identifying these kit homes can be tricky, even for us seasoned pros!

Sears offered its kit homes in many architectural styles, including Foursquares, Spanish Revivals, Neo-Tudors, Colonial Revivals, Cape Cods and Craftsman-style bungalows. (Many people think that Sears created the Craftsman-style bungalow, but this is not correct. The fact that Sears offers an extensive line of "Craftsman" tools seems to add to the confusion.)

The architects and designers at Sears studied the most popular housing styles of the day and worked to emulate those designs. It's *impossible* to identify a Sears house simply by style. You must pay very close attention to the details—large and small—to determine if a particular house is a Sears house. For instance, people get in trouble when they see the catalog picture of the Sears Mitchell and identify it as a Neo-Tudor, and the next time they see a 1930s Neo-Tudor, they decide it's a Sears Mitchell! There are tens of thousands of Neo-Tudors in early twentieth-century neighborhoods, and very few of them are Sears kit homes.

Also, many people believe that they have a Sears kit home because they were told that the building materials arrived in a boxcar. Nevertheless, unless you can match up an existing house with a specific design offered by Sears, you can*not* assume that it is a Sears kit home.

As I've traveled the country studying these houses, I've found that about 75 percent of the people who think they have a Sears kit home are wrong. I've also found well more than three-fourths of the people living in these Sears homes didn't know what they had until I knocked on their door and told them.

So, how *do you* identify a Sears home? First, begin by eliminating the obvious. Sears sold these homes between 1908 and 1940. If your home was built outside of that time frame, it can*not* be a Sears catalog home.

THE LIST OF NINE SIGNS

1. Look for stamped lumber in the basement or attic
2. Look for shipping labels
3. Look for model numbers in blue grease pencil
4. Check house design using original catalogs or a field guide such as this book or *The Houses That Sears Built* or *Houses by Mail*
5. Original documentation
6. Courthouse records
7. Hardware fixtures
8. Goodwall sheet plaster
9. Original building permits

1. Look for marked lumber in the basement or attic. Sears Modern Homes were kit homes, and the framing members were marked with a letter and a three-digit number. When the lumber arrived on site, that number, together with blueprints and an instruction book, told you how all those pieces went together. This mark will be located in two places on each piece of lumber. It will be at the butt end and also on the face of the lumber. Typically, the mark on the face of the lumber can be found two to ten inches from the end of the framing member.

On a two- by eight-inch floor joist, the mark will be on the eight-inch side. Often you can find these marks in the center of the basement, where the butt ends of the floor joists overlap and rest on a center beam. To find it, you'll need a very bright flashlight.

Above: This mark on the floor joists, together with that seventy-five-page instruction book and the detailed blueprints, helped neophyte homebuilders assemble their house. This mark is on the Mohrs' Osborn.

Right: The owners of the Vallonia were so proud of their kit home that they turned the stair treads and risers wrong-side out, revealing the marks on each step.

These marks were in blue, black or red ink and were a little less than an inch in height. If you don't have a basement or don't wish to crawl through the attic, you can also take a peek in the plumbing access door behind the bathtub.

Not all Sears homes have marked lumber. Most Sears homes built before 1920 do not have marked framing members, and a few built after that date have no marks. By 1920, Sears had sold twenty-three thousand houses, so at least one-third do not have marked lumber. The marks are the "low-hanging fruit." It's a fast and easy way to authenticate Sears homes, but its absence does not mean you do not have a Sears home.

2. Look for shipping labels. Shipping labels can often be found on the back of millwork (baseboard molding, door and window trim, etc). The words "Sears Roebuck and Company" will appear on the label, or you might see a return address of 925 Homan Ave, Chicago (Sears headquarters). You might find marks indicating that the lumber was shipped from Norwood Sash and Door in Ohio. This company supplied millwork for Sears homes. If your house contains millwork from Norwood, that doesn't absolutely prove it's a Sears home, but it's a good clue that says "look closer."

3. Look for model numbers scribbled on joists in blue grease pencil. Once the kit home was inventoried, bundled and ready for shipping, the home's model number was written on a floor joist (the largest lumber in the bundle)

Shipping labels can provide a clue that you may have a Sears home. They're usually found on the back of millwork (trim moldings). Often, the words "Sears and Roebuck" don't appear on the shipping label, but rather a return address of 925 Homan Avenue, Chicago, Illinois (Sears headquarters).

Finding a model number scribbled on a joist in blue grease pencil is one way to authenticate a Sears home. Shown here is a floor joist in a Sears Magnolia (also known as Modern Home #2089). These markings are hard to find and require patience, a keen eye and a very bright flashlight.

in blue grease pencil. You'll need a very bright light and keen eyes to spot this, but that blue grease pencil does endure through the decades. After 1918, Sears homes were given names instead of numbers, but the model numbers endured. For instance, the photo shown here is from a Sears Magnolia (built in 1920), model #2089.

4. Find a reference work (such as this book) that shows the home's original floor plan in *detail*. Start with the footprint, or the exterior dimension of the house. If the original floor plan shows a footprint of twenty-six feet by thirty-two feet, the subject house should also be that size. "Almost the same size" doesn't count; it should be precise. Ditto for the dimensions of the individual rooms within the house. Also compare the position of the windows, chimney placement, floor plan, etc. *Finding the Houses That Sears Built* is another good resource (which I highly recommend). It contains the 60 most popular designs. In my experience, those 60 designs represent about 90 percent of the Sears homes that were sold. *Houses by Mail* is another good reference and lists most of the 370 designs that Sears offered.

Room size and floor plan can be a key in authenticating Sears homes. If you have a purported Sears house but can't find marked lumber, look at the room size. It should be a spot-on match to the room sizes listed in *Houses by Mail*. The fraternal twins—houses that look like Sears homes but are not Sears homes—usually do not have identical exterior dimensions, and the sizes of the rooms are tweaked a little bit. Examples are the Sears Mitchell, the Aladdin University and the Gordon Van Tine Patrician. From the exterior, these three houses appear identical, but the exterior dimensions and room sizes were ever-so-slightly different.

Pay special attention to the placement of the furnace chimney. Chimney location is something that (usually) won't be altered even by aggressive remodeling. Fireplaces are a little different. Fireplaces were optional.

These houses were offered in reverse floor plans, so don't be thrown if you find a Sears house that's a mirror image of your home.

5. Look in the attic and basement for any paperwork that might reveal that you have a Sears home. A Sears homeowner in Alton, Illinois, found a complete set of Sears blueprints tucked away in the eaves of her attic, with the words "Honor Bilt" written on the corner of each page. You might peek under the bottom shelf of bookcases and any other nooks and crannies.

6. From 1911 to 1933, Sears offered home mortgages. Using grantee records from the courthouse, you may find a few Sears mortgages and, thus, a few Sears homes. Here's how: look at grantee records from 1915 through 1940. Sears stopped offering mortgages in 1933, but when a mortgage was paid in full, the mortgage release was recorded, so you're going to be looking for that document, as well.

You may find a few Sears mortgages by looking under the name Sears or Sears, Roebuck, but you'll probably find more mortgages by looking under the names Walker O. Lewis and Nicholas Wieland. Both of

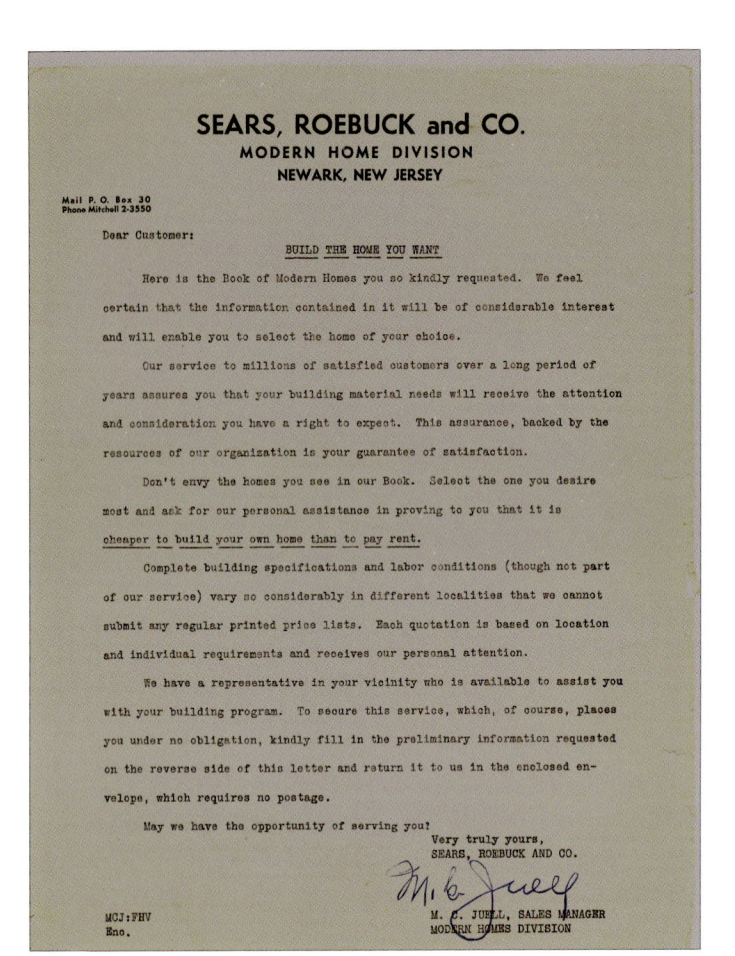

Above: This cover letter came with the 1936 Sears Modern Homes catalog.

Inset at left: Close-up of the Sears Honor Bilt emblem on the Mohrs' blueprints.

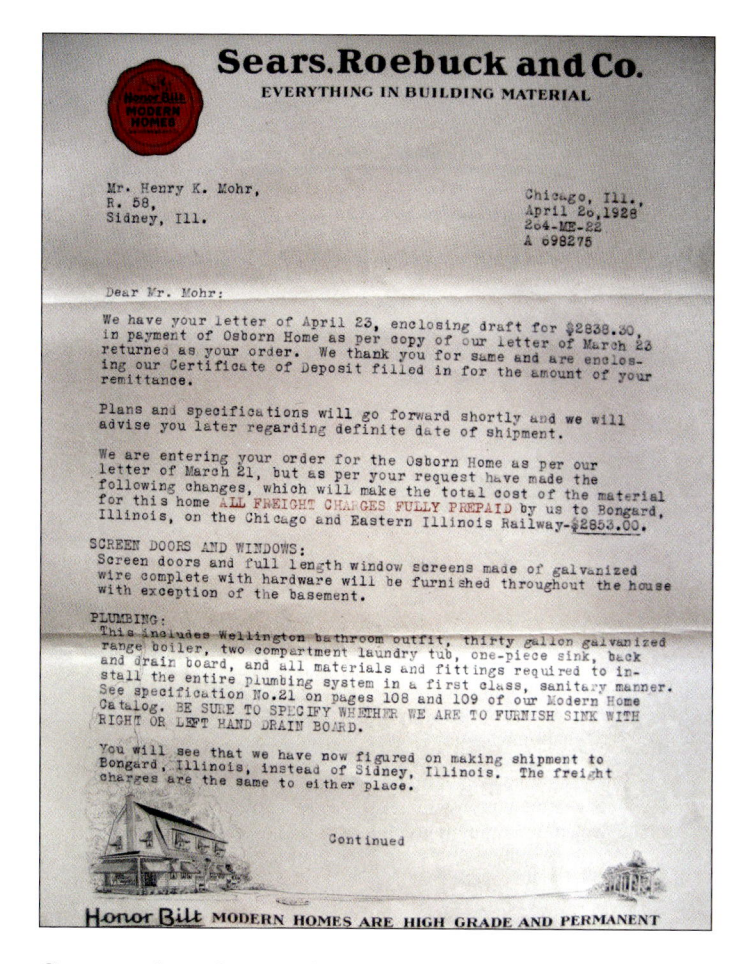

Correspondence between Sears and Henry Mohr.

these men served as trustees for Sears. Walker O. Lewis served as trustee until 1930, when Wieland took over. When you find the names of Lewis or Wieland, you'll probably find the notation "tr," which is an abbreviation for trustee. (Thanks to Dale Patrick Wolicki for the trustee information.)

7. Plumbing, electrical and heating equipment were not included in the basic kit but could be purchased separately. These fixtures were pictured in the back pages of the Sears Modern Homes catalogs and were offered in different grades—good, better and best. This enabled customers to save a little money on their plumbing, heating and lighting fixtures.

Dover Publishing sells a reprint of the 1926 Modern Homes catalog and Schiffer Publishing sells a reprint of the 1912 Modern Homes catalog, which show the type of fixtures that Sears offered. You can also pick up original Modern Homes catalogs from online auction sites, antique stores and flea markets.

Even if the plumbing and electrical equipment in your house has been replaced, the old plumbing fixtures have often migrated to the basement. Compare these old fixtures to the catalog pictures. Also check the plumbing fixtures and see if they bear the initials "SR." Sears homes built during the 1930s often have a small circled "SR" cast into the underside of the sinks (bath and kitchen).

8. Another clue that you have a Sears home is the presence of Goodwall plaster. In the 1910s, Sears

In 2001, Rebecca Hunter and I toured a Vallonia in Columbia, Illinois, that was in mostly original condition. Here's the kitchen—in 2001—looking much like it did when built in 1926.

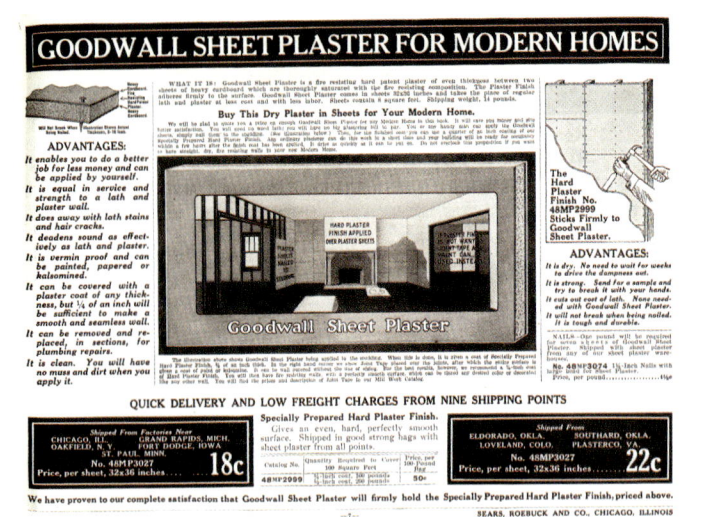

If you find that your home has Goodwall sheet plaster, you may want to investigate further and see if yours is a Sears kit home.

began offering a new product called "sheet plaster" (sheetrock). The Sears product was known as Goodwall Sheet Plaster, and each four-by-four sheet bore the stamp "Goodwall" on the backside. If, during remodeling, you discover this sheet plaster, this suggests that you *may* have a Sears home.

Goodwall Sheet Plaster was also offered in its building materials catalog, so it's not absolute conclusive proof that you have a Sears home. Goodwall Sheet Plaster was never very popular, so most Sears homes do not have it. The overwhelming majority of homes built in the early years of the twentieth century had lath and plaster walls.

9. In Washington, D.C., Mary Rowse (local historian) discovered that Sears Roebuck was occasionally listed as the *architect* on original building permits. It will be interesting to find out if this technique works in other cities, as well. In one county in Illinois, the words "House supplied by Sears Roebuck" appeared on an old city plat.

Some Additional Notes on Identifying Sears Homes

In 1895, Sears began selling lumber, construction supplies, building materials and hardware. Some homebuilders used Sears lumber, hardware and fixtures, which might make it difficult to distinguish a true catalog home from a home built with Sears building materials.

A 1912 promotional booklet (titled *Successful Building: A Book Written by Our Customers*) has a testimonial from a builder that states, "I build suburban residences and two years ago, I commenced using Sears Roebuck and Co.'s building materials, millwork, hardware, mantels, furnaces, ranges, etc."

Is it a Sears house if it is made entirely of materials from Sears? In my estimation, no. It is a Sears home if it was built from plans and blueprints offered in the Sears Modern Homes catalog *and* if the building materials were part of a kit home package offered by Sears.

Old Houses and Big Changes

Learning how to identify Sears homes is a lot like birdwatching, but infinitely more enjoyable! One difference is, you'll never see a yellow-bellied sap sucker covered in aluminum siding. Whether you're looking for a Sears house or a tufted titmouse, you'll need to study and memorize the different styles and then *start looking*!

In Madison County (where I lived for many years), fewer than 10 percent of the Sears homes retain their original siding. You must train your eyes and mind to look *beyond* the contemporary siding materials and "unsee" the changes a home may have endured in the last several decades.

Porches get closed in and new porches are added. Roofs get raised. Houses get additions. Windows disappear, and front doors get moved to the left or right. Or maybe to the side. Yet observing window and door placement is a key element in identifying a potential Sears home. While you're comparing a 1923 foursquare in Jerseyville, Illinois, to the Gladstone, pause and think about the evolution of windows in a typical ninety-year-old house.

When bathtubs are converted into shower enclosures, bathroom windows get yanked and replaced with a solid wall. Many Sears homes had closet windows. (Remember, electricity was in its infancy at the turn of the twentieth century, and closet windows were a big plus in an otherwise dark closet.) These small closet windows are usually the first casualties of substitute sidings.

Sears offered bathroom-less houses from 1908 through the 1930s. Bathrooms (fortunately) are added to these old

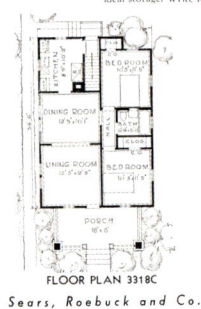

The Crafton was one of Sears's bestsellers, even in the depths of the Great Depression. Today, these houses are especially difficult to identify because they're so simple and small. Oftentimes, extensive remodeling and room additions make identification even more problematic. This happy little yellow Crafton lives in Wood River.

houses in later years. And then windows are added to new bathrooms.

Attic windows get covered by vinyl siding or replaced with louvered vents. Kitchens get enlarged. Pantries (and their windows) disappear. Kitchens and baths endure the most remodeling through the years, and their windows are frequently altered. Big windows get converted into bay or bow windows, and those new windows might not bear the slightest resemblance to the old windows. And that glorious vinyl siding covers it all.

Final Thoughts

If you want to get serious about finding Sears homes, here are some tips.

Study this book. Familiarize yourself with these houses and pay attention to the details that differentiate a Sears Foursquare from any other Foursquare. Keep a copy of this book in your car and use it when you think you've spotted "a suspect." Learn to look at your community's housing stock with new eyes.

Visit an area with a large collection of Sears homes, such as Wood River (with twenty-three in a row on Ninth Street) or Elgin, Illinois, and you'll learn a lot about Sears homes in a hurry. Seeing these houses "in the flesh" will be a boon to your house-hunting career.

Try studying the bigger, fancier homes first. The little houses, like the Winona and the Grant, are so simple that they're difficult to identify. There is little to distinguish these front-gabled cottages from the thousands of small, plain homes that line every modest street in America.

Focus on neighborhoods that were developed in the 1920s (the heyday for Sears homes). Start looking on streets that were less than two miles from the train tracks. Hauling twelve thousand pieces of house by horse and wagon took quite a bit of time, and because of this, these houses often ended up close to the old tracks.

Pay attention to street names. Tree names (Elm, Oak and Maple) were very popular names in the first years of the twentieth century, as were presidential names. Numbered streets were also popular (Second, Third and Fourth Streets). World War I names—both personal names (Pershing Street) and battle names (Vimy Ridge)—were also quite popular in neighborhoods of the 1920s. Look for streets that are laid out in grid patterns. Curvilinear streets and cul-de-sacs didn't become popular until after World War II.

Publicity (newspaper stories and local radio shows) can teach people how to search their homes for stamped lumber, blueprints in the attic, shipping labels on lumber, etc. Such publicity often sparks personal reminiscences, which can help find Sears and other mail-order homes. The window of opportunity for finding these homes through personal reminiscence is fast closing. The people who built these homes have passed on, and even the people who remember helping Mom and Dad build these homes are quite elderly. And yet these people are our best resource for finding the hidden treasure-trove of Sears homes that exist in Illinois.

Chapter 6
Frequently Asked Questions

After my first book on Sears homes was published in March 2002, I hit the road and started giving lectures. Since that time, I've visited twenty-three states and given more than two hundred lectures. After my talk, I open up the floor to questions, and I usually hear the same two dozen questions. Here are my two dozen answers.

How did you get interested in Sears homes?

I was born and raised in Portsmouth, Virginia, in a beautiful neighborhood filled with early twentieth-century homes. I spent countless hours riding my bike through the different neighborhoods, studying and comparing the wide variety of architecture. I have always had a deep abiding love for old homes.

In 1987, I discovered *The Comfortable House*, by Alan Gowans, which was filled with information on kit homes. I read this wonderful book several times. I was in love. While working as a freelance writer in 1999, I asked my editors if they'd like an article about the Sears homes in Carlinville, Illinois. They said yes.

As I started doing research on this topic, I became ever more enchanted with the whole story. In subsequent days (and subsequent trips), I found myself spending hours upon hours at the Carlinville Public Library, reading countless newspaper and magazine articles about the building of those 156 Sears houses in Carlinville's "Standard Addition." Some days, I made the one-hour trip to Carlinville just so that I could plop down on the curb and sit smack dab in the middle of those twelve blocks of Sears homes. The houses made me happy. I loved being in their presence. I loved learning about them. I loved thinking about them. Before long, I'd invested fifty hours in a single article.

I've heard it said that we find our life's work at the place where our personal talents intersect with the world's need for more truth (information) or more beauty or more love. For me, that intersection of my talent and the world's need was a book about Sears homes.

Do you live in a Sears home?

Unfortunately, no. In 1996, our family moved from southeastern Virginia to Alton, Illinois, where we purchased a one-hundred-year-old "handyman special." For the next few years, we devoted ourselves to restoring the old house. In attempting to do a faithful restoration, I learned how difficult (and costly) it is to bring a badly remuddled house back to its original condition. When I speak with passion about the need to restore these Sears homes to their original condition, I speak from experience. In spring 2006, I moved back to Virginia, and today I live in a 1925 Colonial Revival that bears a stunning resemblance to the Sears Lexington.

Would you marry for a Sears home?

Okay, so this is not a *frequently asked question*, but it is a question I was asked at a lecture in central Illinois. And I thought it was a great question, so I include it here. After a fine-looking gentleman asked me this, I paused for a moment and repeated his question: "Would I marry for a Sears home?"

"I guess it depends," I answered thoughtfully. "Which *model* are we talking about?"

If I had met a nice single man who lived in a Sears Magnolia, well, that'd be a strong selling point in his favor. From 2002 to 2006, I had seventy first dates, and one of the most important questions I'd asked those prospective suitors was this: tell me a little something about your house.

You know those thumbnail profile pictures that people post at Internet dating sites? I kept hoping to find a man who would post a picture of his house. In early 2007, I married a man who owned a 1960s condo. *That* was a surprise.

Do you think there's an undiscovered treasure-trove of Sears homes in Illinois? Maybe one that'll trump Elgin's two hundred Sears homes?

Anything's possible, but at this point, I doubt it. Rebecca Hunter (the architectural historian who completed the research in Elgin) and Dale Wolicki (fellow researcher and co-author of *California's Kit Homes* and *Montgomery Ward's Mail-Order Homes*) have visited dozens and dozens of cities in Illinois. Between Rebecca's extensive travels and Dale's extensive travels and my own extensive travels throughout Illinois, I doubt there are going to be any enormous surprises at this point. However, I could be wrong.

Why did Sears stop selling houses?

Sears closed its Modern Homes department once and for all in 1940, partly because of the Depression and poor sales, but there were other factors. When Sears opened its Modern Homes department in 1908, many folks probably remembered helping Mother and Father (or Grandma and Grandpa) build their log cabin or soddie on the family homestead. Building one's own home was an important part of America's heritage, especially in the wide-open spaces of the nineteenth-century Midwest.

By the 1930s, homes had become far more complex. Even modest homes now had plumbing, electricity, central heating systems and more. Homebuilding was increasingly becoming a technical trade, requiring not only contractors but subcontractors and their unique skills and expertise. And when World War II ended (1945), American ideas about building would undergo another major shift, with developers like former U.S. Navy Seabee Bill Levitt, who turned a one-thousand-acre potato field into a neighborhood full of 750-square-foot homes.

And Sears did sell Homart Homes (small prefabricated homes) after World War II, but 1940 seems to have been the end of the Sears Modern Homes department and its kit homes.

How many of these homes are still standing?

While doing research for this book, Rebecca Hunter and I traveled together through several suburbs in northern Illinois. When we came into Glen Ellyn, Rebecca discovered that three Sears homes on one street had been demolished since 2003. This has got to stop. In addition to teardowns, other bad things can happen to good houses, such as fires and street widenings. It's hard to know how many Sears homes remain upright and intact, but I'd guesstimate that perhaps 85 to 90 percent of them are still with us.

Didn't Montgomery Ward also sell homes through its catalogs?

Yes, Montgomery Ward also sold kit homes through its mail-order catalogs. Montgomery Ward began offering kit-home catalogs in 1909, and its last catalog (Wardway Homes) was issued in 1932. Unlike Sears, Montgomery Ward did not have an architectural staff devoted to its Modern Homes department. Gordon Van Tine supplied the kit homes (and catalogs) and handled order fulfillment for Wardway. For more information, read *Montgomery Ward's Mail-Order Homes* by Wolicki and Thornton.

What about the other companies that offered houses by mail order?

Aladdin Homes of Bay City, Michigan, was probably Sears's largest competitor in the kit home business. Two brothers, William and Otto Sovereign, started their kit home business in 1906 (two years before Sears). Aladdin Homes closed in 1981, having sold more than seventy-five thousand kit homes.

The other major contender in the kit home business was Gordon Van Tine. Based in Davenport, Iowa, this company sold about fifty to sixty thousand homes.

Lewis Manufacturing went into the building materials business in 1896 and started selling kit homes in 1913. In the mid-'20s, it changed its name to Liberty Homes and continued in business until 1973, selling about 50,000 homes.

Pacific Ready-Cut Homes sold about forty thousand houses along the West Coast. There was also Harris Brothers (formerly known as the Chicago House Wrecking Company), R.L. Bennett, Sterling Homes and countless regional companies.

National Refrigerators, a St. Louis company that manufactured and sold wooden iceboxes, issued a kit house catalog in the late 1910s called Miller Ready-Built Homes offering some of the most nondescript cottages and bungalows that you ever saw. Almost every sizeable community had a regional kit home company for a time. (Thanks to Dale Patrick Wolicki for the information on Aladdin, Gordon Van Tine, Lewis-Liberty and Miller Ready-Built Homes.)

I found some marks on the framing members of my old house, but they're several numbers separated by a hyphen. What does that mean?

The marked lumber on houses sold by Gordon Van Tine (and Montgomery Ward) looked a little different than Sears. Gordon Van Tine used several digits separated by a hyphen, such as 17-23-18. I've also seen a *word* stamped on each individual board, describing the placement of the lumber or board, such as "dormer roof" or "rafter."

Are any companies still selling kit homes today?

Yes. Log homes are the popular kit homes today, but there are also several regional companies selling conventional kit homes. To find them, look up "kit homes" on the Internet. However, I seriously doubt they'll send you a full set of blueprints for one dollar, as Sears once did.

What was the final cost of a Sears kit home?

The 1922 Sears Modern Homes catalog had an extra bit of information I've not seen in other Modern Homes catalogs. It listed "built complete" prices. For instance, the

Puritan cost $1,947, but Sears added this in small print: "Can be BUILT COMPLETE with plumbing, high grade warm air heating plant, electric wiring and lighting fixtures, including all material and all labor, for $4888."

The Betsy Ross cost $1,504, but the "built complete" price was $4,340. The Avondale was $2,685, but the complete price was $6,250. The price of the house, multiplied by a factor of 2.3 to 3.0, would give a better idea of the "built complete" cost.

Why were the house prices so low?

The prices Sears quoted for these houses were for the building materials *alone*. Wages in the 1910s and 1920s were a fraction of today's incomes. According to *American Carpenter and Builder Magazine* (December 1912), skilled carpenters in Chicago were earning sixty-five cents an hour and plumbers were making seventy-five cents an hour.

How much money did people save by buying and building a kit home?

It's tough to say for sure, but apparently, you'd save about one-third by building your own kit home. Some of the kit home companies claimed homebuyers would save up to 50 percent by building kit homes, but so much probably depended on the local economies.

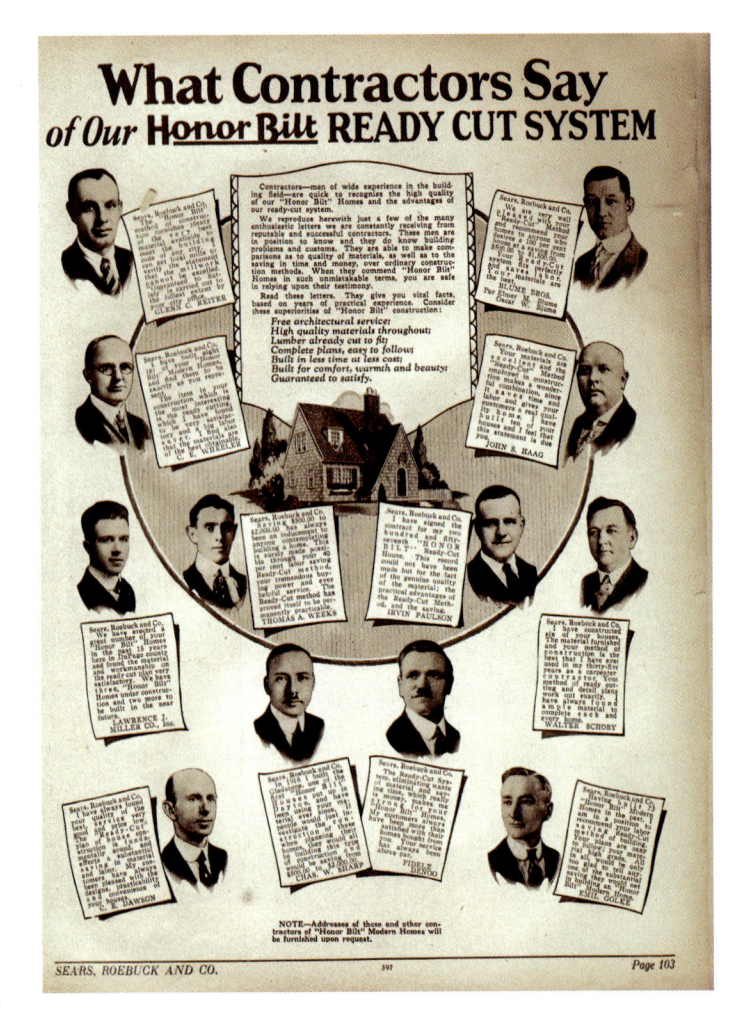

Sears kit homes were very popular with contractors, too, as is shown by this promotion in the 1928 catalog.

64

Did Sears build these houses, too? Did it offer construction services?

In the beginning, no, Sears only sold the kit homes. However, in the late 1920s, it began to offer construction help. In *Business Week* on March 26, 1930, there was an article entitled "Quality Production Reaches the Home Builder." It discussed this new construction service offered by both Sears and Wards, stating, "About all the customer has to do is to say, 'Build me such and such a house on such and such a lot.' The company does the rest."

The article went on to say that this new service was already proving to be "exceedingly popular." Both Wards and Sears offered the homebuilder as much or as little help as he wanted or needed with construction of the kit home.

How many people built these Sears homes themselves?

Judging from the testimonials (an admittedly unscientific method), it would seem that about half the Sears homes were built by the homeowners and half were built by professional carpenters and builders. By the way, when I'm researching a purported Sears home and I find that the original owner was a carpenter, I always heave a little sigh. Frequently, the kit homes built by carpenters were *significantly* altered from the original designs and plans.

Bold promises of "easy payments" and "lowest interest" graced the cover of the 1930 catalog.

If a house has an "S" on the chimney, does that mean it is a Sears home?

This nutty (albeit persistent) rumor has been floating around for years now. Every now and then, the occasional reporter asks me if this is true. It is not true! That wrought-iron "S" you see on the chimney of the occasional Tudor Revival is a stylistic element that has no relation to the Sears Modern Homes department. None.

Did Sears have a "dollar a knot" guarantee on the lumber in its kit homes?

It was Aladdin—not Sears—that promised buyers a silver dollar if they found a knot bigger than a dime in their framing lumber. Aladdin's 1919 catalog stated: "The lumber in Aladdin Readi-Cut Houses is higher in grade throughout than any regularly carried by any seller in America. Further, we guarantee that you will receive clear and knotless siding, clear and knotless flooring, clear and knotless interior finish, for every Aladdin dwelling house."

Where did you get your old Sears Modern Home catalogs and how much did they cost?

In the last several years, I've purchased these catalogs through online auction sites and from online antiquarian

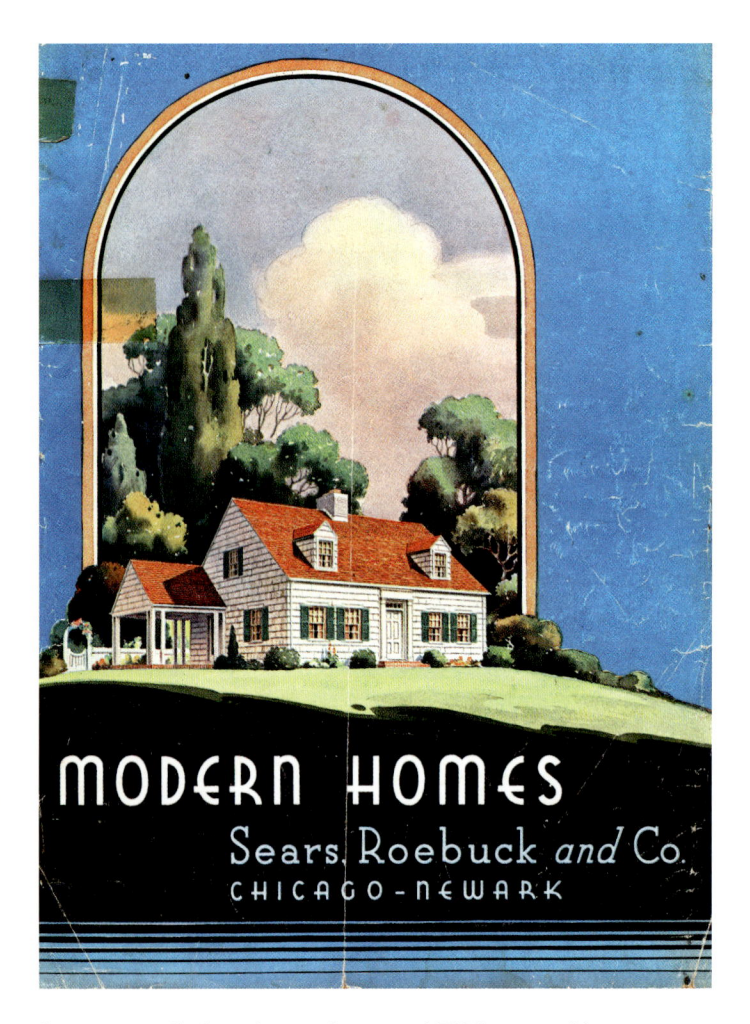

Sears now relied on the newly created FHA to provide mortgage money for its kit homes, and the cover of the 1938 catalog is surprisingly bereft of "easy money" promises. The Attleboro sits serenely in the background.

The 1909 Modern Homes catalog is extremely rare and hard to find. The cover shows a tree-lined street full of Sears Modern Homes.

book dealers. Prices for the original catalogs are fifty dollars and up. For about fifteen dollars, you can buy a reprint of the 1926 Sears Modern Homes catalog from Dover Publishing. Schiffer Publishing also offers a good quality reprint of the 1912 Sears Modern Homes catalog. Both are available at Amazon.com.

What about those little houses with tile walls and metal roofs—are they Sears homes?

It's amazing how many people think that prefab steel houses are Sears homes. Many of the steel homes with "tile walls" are Lustron Homes, post–World War II prefabricated homes. Lustrons were made of twenty-gauge porcelain enamel steel tiles, and each tile measured two by two feet. The interior walls also were steel tile. If you wanted to hang a picture on the wall, you didn't use nails—you used magnets! There are only a few thousand Lustron Homes in the country, and they're concentrated in the Midwest. *Lustron was not connected to Sears*. To learn more about Lustrons, read *Lustron Homes* by Tom Fetters.

What about Sears kit barns?

In the 1909 Sears Modern Homes catalog, a single sentence appeared that stated, "Our architects are now preparing plans for several designs of good substantial up to date barns for which we will be able to furnish plans about July 1, 1910."

The 1918 Sears "Book of Barns" stated, "The much discussed difficult task of barn building has been reduced by us to a pleasing undertaking. If during the construction of your barn, you should fail to understand some detail, which is unlikely with our proved 'Already Cut' system, write us, stating just what the difficulty is. We will promptly set you right."

Sears barns were offered in traditional shapes (rectangular), but it also offered L-shaped barns, round barns and octagonal barns. And Sears sold every other outbuilding imaginable, including silos, poultry houses, hog houses, icehouses, milk houses, outhouses and more.

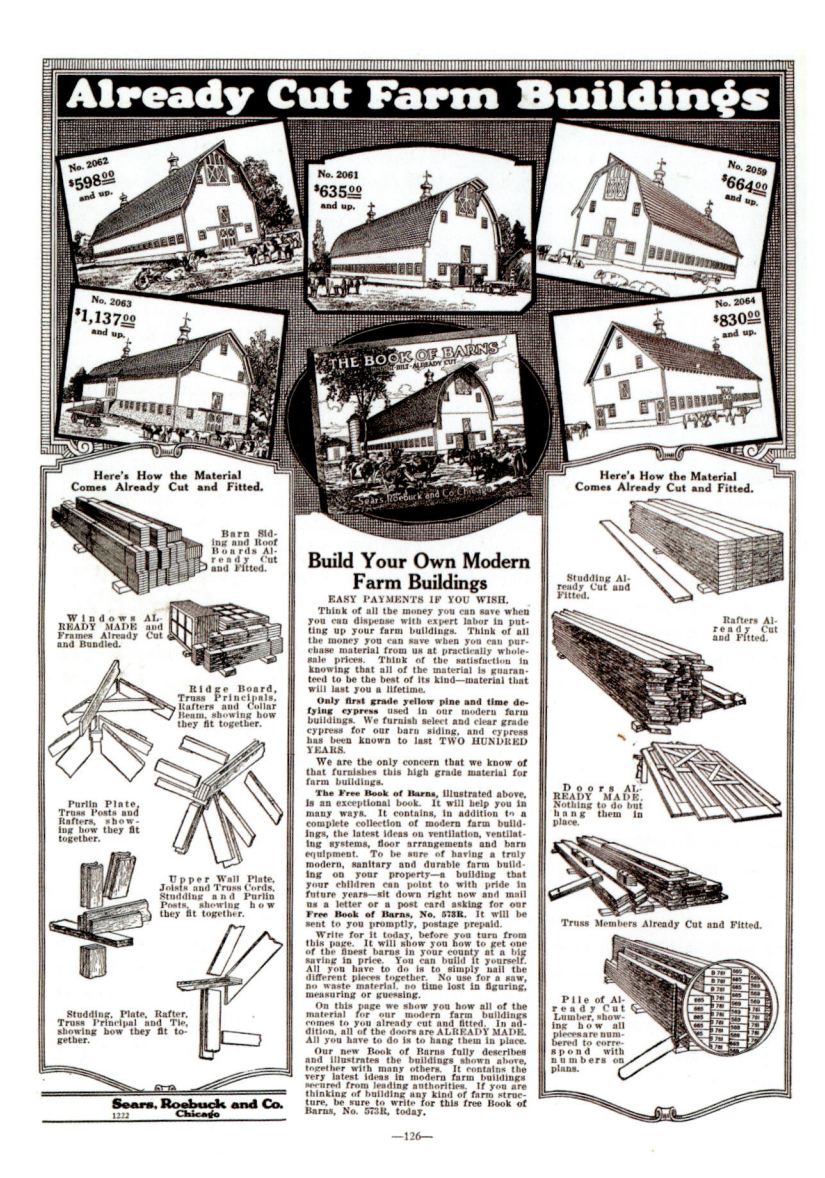

Above: This well-kept Sears barn sits on a spacious farm with a Sears house (the Gladstone). Lightning rods adorn the peak on its original tin roof. (Mattoon)

Left: The 1919 Sears Modern Homes catalog had a full-page spread promoting its "Modern Farm Buildings," which were "already cut," meaning that all the framing members for the barn arrived pre-cut and ready to be nailed into place.

Do Sears homes have more value than traditional stick-built homes?

That's a tough question to answer. I think it depends on the community and the local economy. In many parts of Illinois, where Sears homes are so common and real estate prices are so low, I don't think the "Sears home" designation automatically makes a house more valuable.

I always suspected that my parents' house was a Sears home because I remember when it came in on the railroad and my brother and I helped our parents unload the boxcars. Are you sure their house isn't a Sears home?

This also is a very common question. People often show me photos of their "Sears home," and about 75 percent of the time, I have to tell them, "That is a lovely home, but it is *not* a design of a Sears home that I recognize." And that simple statement could mean several things. It's possible that their Sears home was extensively customized, in which case I tell the letter writers to look for shipping labels, stamped lumber, blue grease pencil marks, etc.

More frequently, I discover that their home is a design that was offered by another kit home company. These many years later, folks have forgotten the name of the other national kit home companies, such as Gordon Van Tine, Aladdin, Sterling Homes, Lewis Homes and Harris Brothers. However, they do remember that the house came in a kit and was shipped by boxcar. "Sears home" has become a generic name for *all* kit homes. Fewer than 25 percent of the photos I receive are readily recognizable as Sears kit homes.

What are some common misconceptions about Sears homes?

Many people have the idea that Sears homes are lesser-quality homes and/or they're very modest homes. Sears *did* sell "Simplex Cottages," which were true prefabs (shipped in sections to be bolted together at the site), and these were very small, modest houses that were considered temporary or portable. These homes probably didn't survive more than a few years. However, the bread and butter of the Sears Modern Home's program—the Honor Bilt home—was a remarkably solid house and came in hundreds of different designs, shapes and sizes.

Occasionally, I'm asked if these Sears homes are as solid as traditional stick-built houses, since it was often the homeowner who fulfilled the "some assembly required" component. My answer is, *absolutely*. It's been my experience that when someone is creating something for the first time and for their own family, they tend to be zealots, making sure everything is "just so" and perfect. Whether it's creating meatloaf for the family meal or building a home, it's human nature to have the highest standards for those in our innermost circle.

The blueprints and instructions that came with your Sears kit home were incredibly detailed and even specified proper spacing of those 750 pounds of nails. Sears's promise was bold but true—"If you follow these instructions, you can *not* make a mistake."

Years ago, I wrote an article about Habitat for Humanity and learned that during Hurricane Andrew in 1993, the modest homes built by Habitat withstood the hurricane, while the more expensive homes succumbed to the high winds. There are two reasons for this. One, Habitat Homes were built by volunteers and homeowners and they worked slowly, carefully and thoughtfully. For instance, they used hammers instead of nail guns. If a nail missed the framing member, the volunteer would stop, pull the nail out of the sheathing and try again. When a nail gun misses the framing, the construction worker keeps on walking across the roof, popping in nail after nail. Novices also tend to overbuild and use more nails than are necessary. It seems likely that these same principles applied to the building of Sears kit homes.

How can I educate the folks in my community as to the value of Sears homes?

Identify a few Sears homes in your community and then contact the owners and tell them all about it. Use public forums! Read this book a few dozen times and you'll be prepared to address your city council and historical societies. Contact the local media and try to get newspaper articles written about the Sears homes in your city; put together a few museum exhibits; contact the local civic groups and offer to give a short talk at a luncheon, etc.

The window of opportunity for finding Sears homes through personal reminiscences is fast closing. The people who built these Sears homes, for the most part, have passed on. Even the people who remember helping Mom and Dad build a kit house are quite elderly. I think it's imperative to find these people and record their stories (and learn about their Sears homes) before *they* pass on.

Chapter 7
Conclusion

It was 1928 when twelve-year-old Muriel Mohr came home from school to find the charred remnants of the family homestead. It must have been devastating. However, I suspect that Muriel—like most young people would—was watching her parents to see how they responded to such an unthinkable tragedy. And I suspect that Henry and Ethel Mohr understood that this experience was a teachable moment. They were teaching their young daughter—by their own example—how to keep going forward when life deals you an unfair blow.

Despite the fact that they lost their house and most of its furnishings, Henry and Ethel did not throw in the towel and give up on their piece of the American dream. These second-generation Americans were not about to walk away from the plot of ground they'd spent years nurturing and cultivating and farming. They weren't about to give up on the 160-acre Illinois homestead that Henry's parents—Frederick and Wilhelmina Mohr—had homesteaded when they emigrated from Germany. By 1928, Henry and Ethel and Frederick and Wilhelmina had seventy-four years invested in this patch of fertile midwestern farmland.

In 1928, the Henry Mohrs turned to Sears Roebuck to transform their burden into a blessing, and that blessing took the shape of a beautiful little red and white bungalow that would endure for generations to come.

Building that house for his family, I'm confident that Henry and his brother-in-law Frank paid close attention to each and every detail in that seventy-five-page instruction book and the accompanying blueprints. I'd bet money that when the Mohrs built their Sears Osborn, they knew it would be a house that would outlive them and their children.

When Muriel Mohr married Dean Riggs in 1939, they took their vows in the Osborn's living room. After the war, Muriel and Dean moved into a little house on the edge of the Mohrs' farmstead. Muriel and Dean's two children, Dennis and Linda, grew up in that little house. Dennis and Linda had only to scurry through a grove of fruit trees to visit Grandma and Grandpa's house. In 1975, Ethel passed on, and exactly two months later, Henry followed her. Muriel inherited the Osborn, and in 1978, she and her husband moved into the house her father built.

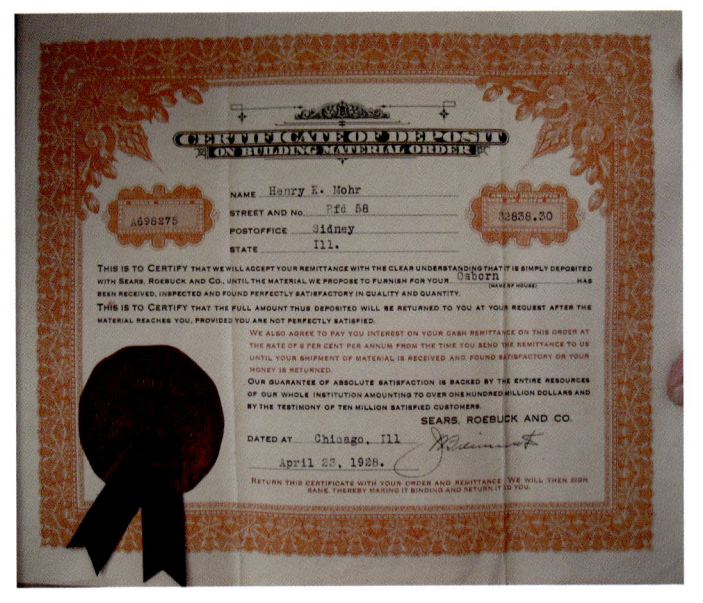

Above, left: The Mohrs' Osborn on a three-hundred-acre farm, just south of Sidney.

Above, right: The Mohrs' home came with a certificate of deposit, showing that the Mohrs' money would remain on deposit with Sears until their Osborn had been delivered and inventoried.

Left: This board probably was saved from the wooden shipping crate that brought Henry and Ethel Mohr their Honor Bilt Sears Osborn in 1928. "Bongard" was the name of the rail yard where the house was delivered.

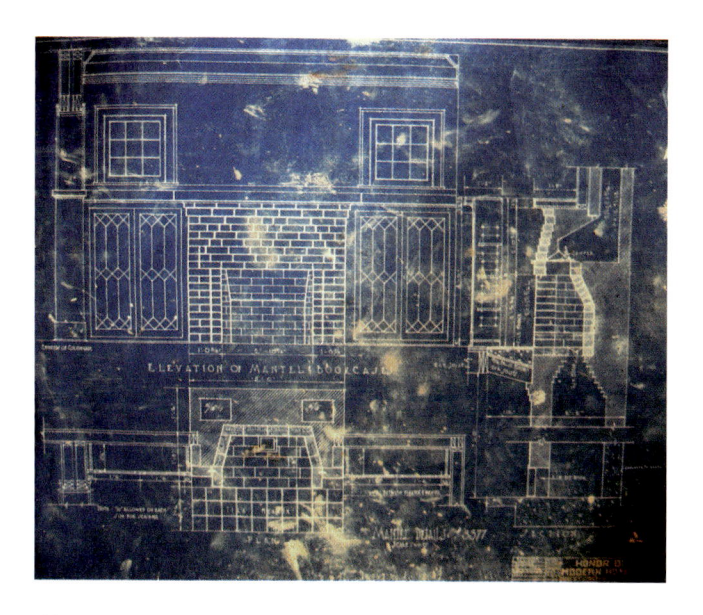

Above, left: Detail on the blueprint, showing the fireplace and surrounding area.

Above, right: Interior of the Mohrs' Osborn, showcasing the fireplace mantel, bookcases and small windows. The stained-glass windows are not original to the house.

The architectural historian in me thinks back to 1928, where I can imagine Muriel's father putting the finishing touches on their fine, new modern home. I can picture Henry Mohr pausing from his work to explain the import of this house to his little girl. Maybe he took her twelve-year-old hands in his wizened, calloused hands, looked into her eyes and said, "I built this house for you, and for your children, and for their children. Always remember, if you could see a father's love, it would look like just this house: strong, true and enduring."

Since 2002, I've been interviewed hundreds of times by hundreds of reporters in too many cities to count. After the story appears in print or on television, reporters consistently tell me that their piece on Sears homes generated more viewer/reader response than *any story they've ever done*. There's a reason for that, and the Riggses' story helped me better understand the reason.

There's so much more to this story than kit homes sold out of a mail-order catalog. Each and every home is a piece of the tapestry that is the fabric of America and its

Left: Original light fixture in the Mohrs' home.

Below: Picture from the 1928 catalog showing the light fixture.

Above: Close-up of the Narcissus design hardware that the Mohrs chose for their Osborn.

Left: Detail of the Sears Narcissus hardware in the Mohrs' home.

74

people and its success. Homesteaders and city dwellers alike worked and struggled and strived to improve their lot in life and to create a better life for themselves and their children and their children's children. They were willing to give up a year's wages to secure a piece of land, and they were willing to place an order for twelve thousand pieces of building material from a large mail-order company in Chicago, Illinois, and then—working nights and weekends—assemble those pieces into something that resembled a house.

The Riggses' family story, multiplied thousands of times, gives a thumbnail sketch of the story of Illinois and the story of our country. In the first years of the twentieth century, magazines and newspapers of the day consistently promoted this message: It's your patriotic *duty* to become a homeowner. The early Sears Modern Homes catalogs stated this basic philosophy in different ways, but there was an elementary core truth therein: Homeowners have a vested interest in their community, and communities with a large percentage of homeowners will enjoy a greater proportion of prosperity, stability and peace.

In one of my favorite movies, *It's a Wonderful Life*, George Bailey gets to see what his town, Bedford Falls, would have looked like if he'd never been born. Without George's positive influence and his struggling Building and Loan, the modern subdivision of Bailey Park would never have been developed and countless citizens would never have had the opportunity to become homeowners.

Without the Bailey Building and Loan, George finds that Bedford Falls is full of substandard rental properties. And because there are so many rental properties, there is less stability in the family structure, and in a broader context, there is less stability in the whole community. In this alternate sans-George world, Ernie the cabdriver does not live with his family in their own "nice little home in Bailey Park," but instead, his home is a decrepit shack in Pottersville, and it's implied that this hardship is partly to blame for the fact that Ernie's wife "ran off three years ago and took the kid."

The streets of this alternate Bedford Falls (now named Pottersville) are lined with liquor stores, nightclubs, pawnbrokers, striptease shows and pool halls. Gaudy neon signs flash "girls, girls, girls" and illumine the nighttime corridors of Main Street. Citizens are neither calm nor law-abiding, and brusque policemen struggle to keep peace and order.

George's revelation that he really had a "wonderful life" stemmed in part from the realization that his meager efforts to give people the chance to become homeowners gave them a feeling of accomplishment, prosperity, security and pride. By extension, the whole community benefited in important, significant and enduring ways.

Perhaps Sears was to Illinois what George Bailey was to Bedford Falls. Sears empowered and enabled tens of thousands of working-class and immigrant families to build their own homes. What would countless midwestern towns have become without Sears homes? How many towns in the Midwest were spared the fate of becoming a Pottersville? Probably many.

Sears Modern Homes made a significant difference in many communities throughout Illinois and the Midwest. I'm sure of that.

In November 2000, Muriel Mohr Riggs became ill and had to move out of her beloved Osborn, the house her father built. Five years later, she passed on. In spring 2010, I traveled back to Sidney, Illinois, to visit with the Riggs family and learn a little more about the Sears Osborn on the family farm. Muriel's son Dennis was now the proud owner of the Sears Osborn and its crumpled, yellow blueprints. As he and I sat down to breakfast one morning, I asked Dennis if I could take a look at those original blueprints from 1928.

Dennis hesitated for just a second.

"Let's talk for a minute," he said, "and then we'll look at the blueprints."

His mother had taught him well.

The Gallery

What two items in the early 1900s mail-order catalogs made Sears both famous and wealthy? The answer might surprise you: sewing machines and cream separators. Richard Warren Sears was a marketing genius, and he knew that if he could find a way to produce and sell these two essentials for less than ten dollars and twenty-five dollars, respectively, he'd have a hit on his hands.

And he was right. This is what Mr. Sears did best: he paid attention to what people wanted and then figured out how to slice the costs of producing and manufacturing that merchandise, thus making it affordable for the masses.

The same was true for houses. Sears was not an innovator when it came to architectural design. The in-house architects at Sears examined the popular housing styles of the time (Foursquares, Bungalows, Cape Cods, Neo-tudors, Colonial Revivals and Dutch Colonials) and then drafted their own vanilla-flavored version. In the following pages, you'll see the wide variety of styles that Sears offered during its thirty-two years in the kit home business.

These were good houses, and they were (with few exceptions) attractive, practical, thoughtfully designed and made good use of small spaces. However, many of these kit homes blend right in with their surrounding neighbors, lacking distinctive architectural details that would distinguish them from other homes. It takes a sharp and discerning eye to differentiate an early 1930s Neo-Tudor from the Sears Mitchell or to figure out if that mid-1910s Foursquare came out of the Sears catalog or was erected by a local builder.

It also takes a little practice and persistence to learn how to distinguish Sears kit homes from stick-built housing, but there are few things in life that are more enjoyable than studying this fascinating piece of our country's architectural heritage. *Sears Homes of Illinois* is a key to the hidden treasure-trove of kit homes in your community that are just waiting to be rediscovered and cherished and enjoyed.

Have fun finding these architectural treasures.

Cape Cod

In 1930, housing starts began to fall throughout the country (due to the Great Depression). And for this reason, post-1930 Sears homes can be hard to find. Sears didn't offer Cape Cod–style homes until the late 1920s, and yet Attleboros, Concords and Lorains were some of its bestselling houses in these post-Depression years. All three of these Cape Cod homes had bedrooms on the first floor, with an expandable attic on the upper floor, making the house very appealing for the budget-conscious, growing family. For nearly four hundred years, the ubiquitous Cape Cod has been a popular housing style in America. And these Attleboros, Concords and Lorains were surprisingly popular for Sears.

THE ATTLEBORO
SIX ROOMS — BATH AND LAVATORY

MODERN HOME
No. 3384
ALREADY CUT AND FITTED

THIS type of Cape Cod home is one of the first designs built by the early New England settlers. Homes built over a hundred years ago grow old gracefully and still retain a certain warmth and beauty. It seems to have many friends in both urban and suburban areas. The Attleboro achieves distinction with its fine doorway, dormers, shuttered windows and correct architectural details. No "gingerbread" to get out of date. Outside walls are shown of Cedar shingles, but will look equally attractive with siding.

FIRST FLOOR PLAN

The first floor lavatory opening off the rear hall, in addition to complete second floor bath, adds greatly to the value. Closets for outer wraps handy to front and rear doors. Central hall with semi-open stairs, large living room, dining room and exceptional kitchen, complete the first floor plan. Double drainboard kitchen sink with built-in cabinets as shown on floor plans are suggested at a slight additional cost.

SECOND FLOOR PLAN

Two large bedrooms and one smaller one, each with a good closet, open off the upstairs hall. Each bedroom is well lighted and contains good wall space. A hall closet for linens at the left of the bath is a real convenience. The bathroom plumbing "roughs in" directly over the kitchen which reduces installation cost. Three attractive "Aristocrat" plumbing fixtures as available in Specification 22B work out nicely in the bath. A built-in Venetian mirrored medicine case is part of the standard equipment furnished with this home.

The floor plan is 36 ft. wide by 26 ft. deep and will require a 60-foot lot on account of the 11 foot porch at the side. In case of a narrow lot, porch could be placed at the rear of the living room instead of at the side.

Our base price includes all necessary material to build this six-room-and-bath home, consisting of lumber, lath, millwork, flooring, shingles, building paper, hardware, metal and painting material according to complete detail specifications.

Fill out Blank for complete delivered price including heating; lighting and plumbing.

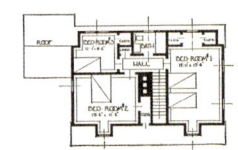

Sears, Roebuck and Co.

SECOND FLOOR PLAN

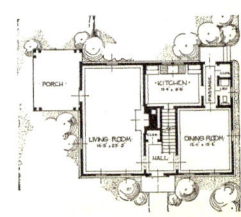

FIRST FLOOR PLAN

The Attleboro is an especially tough house to identify for two reasons: one, the Cape Cod was such a ubiquitous housing style, and two, Cape Cods have few distinguishing features. The Sears Attleboro had a center fireplace chimney and those second-floor dormers, which sit very low on the roofline. Both Rebecca Hunter and I had a chance to inspect this house in Champaign, and we found stamped lumber in the basement, authenticating it as a Sears house.

Cape Cod

CAPE COD

THE CONCORD
FIVE ROOMS, BATH, RECREATION ROOM AND FUTURE BEDROOM

MODERN HOME No. 3379
ALREADY CUT AND FITTED

THE CONCORD is a true American Cape Cod home. Its beautiful exterior and practical floor plan have made it one of America's most popular low-priced homes. The Concord, as offered by Sears, employs a new principle in construction which is a big money saver.

The Plan has four levels. The basement which is just a few feet below grade, requires only a minimum excavation, being confined to the left wing only, but sufficiently large to provide recreation room, laundry and heater room. The recreation room can be converted into an attached garage if desired. (See the garage entrance of the Homestead on opposite page.)

The regular floor level, which is only six steps up from the basement, contains a living room size 19 feet 7 inches by 11 feet 5 inches and dining room size 11 feet 0 inches by 11 feet 5 inches with a spacious closet. A well arranged kitchen is also on this level. A small hall forms the entrance to the basement level and gives additional storage.

A short flight of open stairs with wrought iron rail brings you to the second floor containing two bedrooms, bath, three closets and linen storage. You will note on the topmost level that it is possible to have a third bedroom in the space over the living room.

These two houses are good examples of careful planning and how you can secure seven-room efficiency in the space ordinarily devoted to five rooms.

The quantity and quality of all the materials and equipment for these homes are fully guaranteed by Sears.

See pages 4 and 5 for details on ready cut features.
See pages 12 to 15 for information on heating, lighting and plumbing.

FIRST FLOOR PLAN

SECOND FLOOR PLAN

THE AUBURN
MODERN HOME No. 3382
NOT ALREADY CUT

THE AUBURN Modern Home is another good example of what proper design will accomplish in the way of large convenient rooms in a small area.

The floor plans of the Auburn are the same as the Concord shown above. There is one more closet and a large vestibule formed by the unique front entrance of the Auburn's English architecture.

The exterior walls are treated with a number of different finishes. The front wall under the overhanging gable has perpendicular siding, the vestibule, stucco and half timber, balance of the house, 24-inch shingles.

▶ Page 36 ◀   641   *Modern Homes Division*

The Modern Homes of the mid-1930s are tougher to find, because housing starts dropped sharply during the Great Depression. However, the Concord was one of the most popular 1930s houses. The inset dormer and cantilevered third level are distinctive features. (Nashville)

THE LORAIN

SIX ROOMS AND BATH

MODERN HOME No. 3281 ALREADY CUT AND FITTED

FROM the modern woman's point of view, it is almost impossible to over emphasize the importance and convenience of having a first floor bedroom. It not only comes in handy for guests, but can be furnished to also act as a den or library.

At first glance, few would suppose that this charming Colonial house contained six large, well balanced rooms. You usually view the front entrance first and last and your impression of this should be good as it is well balanced with the rest of the exterior features—shutters on front windows —Colonial siding and circle head dormer. All exterior siding, moldings and trim of clear lumber and all protected with three coats of our famous Master-Mixed paint.

THE FLOOR PLANS

The right side of the first floor plan contains the living room and dining room, connected with wide plaster arch giving the appearance of one large room, size 11 feet 2 in. wide by 29 feet long. The hall which also contains the encased stair to the second floor connects the bedroom, bath and kitchen. You will find plenty of wall space for equipment and kitchen cabinets (furnished at option price) as well as cross ventilation. Refrigeration space is planned under wall cabinet unit next to entrance of grade and cellar stairs.

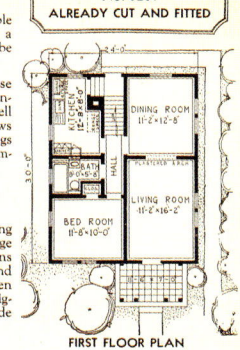

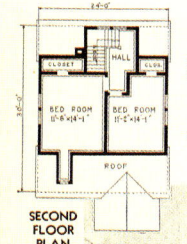

SECOND FLOOR PLAN

A "split roof" type dormer with two windows, gives the necessary head room and light to the upstairs hall, opening from which you will find two large bedrooms and closets.

Select your garage from designs shown on pages 62 and 63.

This "Honor Bilt" home is 24 feet wide and 30 feet deep and can be built on a lot 30 feet wide.

Fill out Blank you will find in the back of this book for complete delivered price.

Sears, Roebuck and Co.

The Lorain is an easy house to pick out—usually—with its distinctive round dormer and matching front porch roof. Notice the two groupings of paired columns and the keystone at the peak of the porch's arch. This Lorain in Elgin has an extra-big dormer, probably added in later years.

CAPE COD

Trailing-Edge Victorian

The Victorian was a well-known housing style, popular in the second half of the 1800s, but "Trailing-edge Victorian" is more a descriptive phrase than an official style. Sears started selling kit homes in 1908, just as interest in Victorian homes had started to wane. It was Pasteur's discovery of the germ theory that dug the grave for the Victorian, with all its germ-hiding fretwork and frippery. The Clyde and the Maytown are best described as "Trailing-edge Victorians" because they're neither ostentatious nor ornate, yet they have the classic lines of the Victorian house.

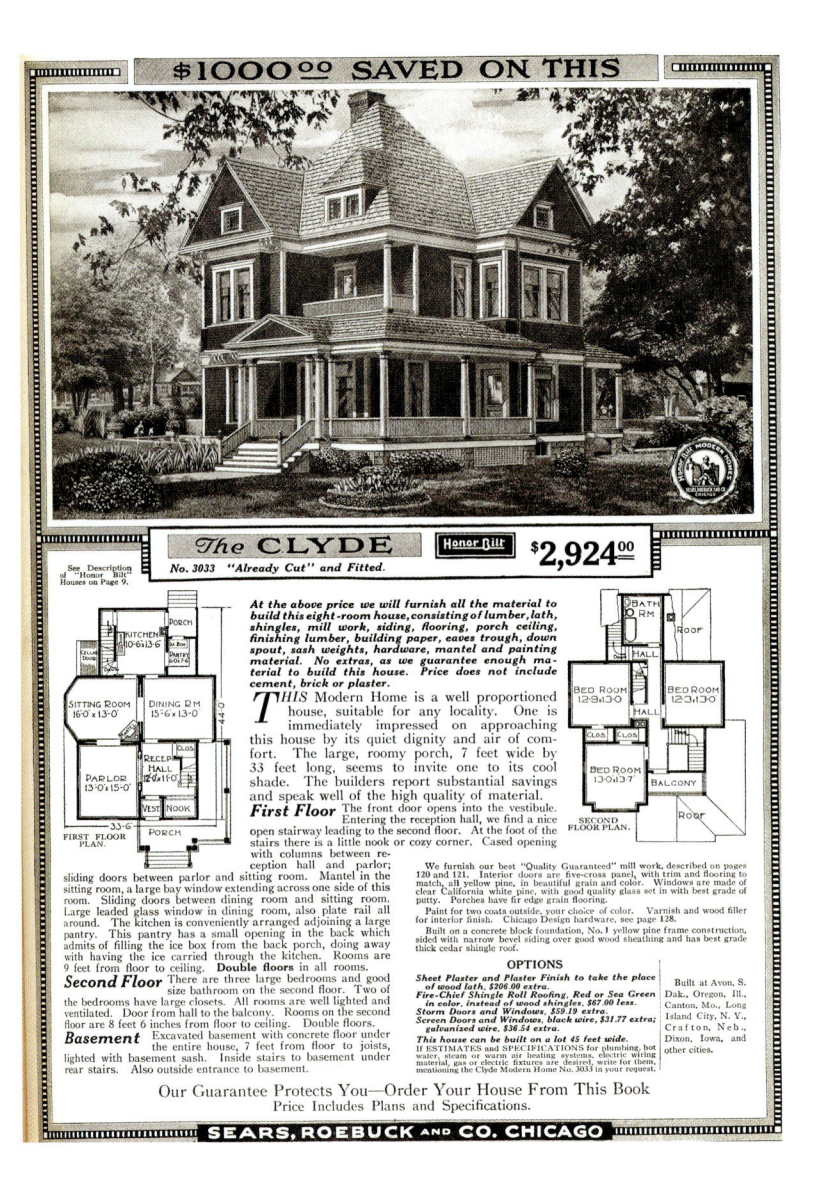

$1000.00 SAVED ON THIS

The CLYDE — Honor Bilt — $2,924.00
No. 3033 "Already Cut" and Fitted.

At the above price we will furnish all the material to build this eight-room house, consisting of lumber, lath, shingles, mill work, siding, flooring, porch ceiling, finishing lumber, building paper, eaves trough, down spout, sash weights, hardware, mantel and painting material. No extras, as we guarantee enough material to build this house. Price does not include cement, brick or plaster.

THIS Modern Home is a well proportioned house, suitable for any locality. One is immediately impressed on approaching this house by its quiet dignity and air of comfort. The large, roomy porch, 7 feet wide by 33 feet long, seems to invite one to its cool shade. The builders report substantial savings and speak well of the high quality of material.

First Floor The front door opens into the vestibule. Entering the reception hall, we find a nice open stairway leading to the second floor. At the foot of the stairs there is a little nook or cozy corner. Cased opening with columns between reception hall and parlor, sliding doors between parlor and sitting room. Mantel in the sitting room, a large bay window extending across one side of this room. Sliding doors between dining room and sitting room. Large leaded glass window in dining room, also plate rail all around. The kitchen is conveniently arranged adjoining a large pantry. This pantry has a small opening in the back which admits of filling the ice box from the back porch, doing away with having the ice carried through the kitchen. Rooms are 9 feet from floor to ceiling. **Double floors** in all rooms.

Second Floor There are three large bedrooms and good size bathroom on the second floor. Two of the bedrooms have large closets. All rooms are well lighted and ventilated. Door from hall to the balcony. Rooms on the second floor are 8 feet 6 inches from floor to ceiling. Double floors.

Basement Excavated basement with concrete floor under the entire house, 7 feet from floor to joists, lighted with basement sash. Inside stairs to basement under rear stairs. Also outside entrance to basement.

We furnish our best "Quality Guaranteed" mill work, described on pages 120 and 121. Interior doors are five-cross panel, with trim and flooring to match, all yellow pine, in beautiful grain and color. Windows are made of clear California white pine, with good quality glass set in with best grade of putty. Porches have fir edge grain flooring.

Paint for two coats outside, your choice of color. Varnish and wood filler for interior finish. Chicago Design hardware, see page 128.

Built on a concrete block foundation, No. 1 yellow pine frame construction, sided with narrow bevel siding over good wood sheathing and has best grade thick cedar shingle roof.

OPTIONS
Sheet Plaster and Plaster Finish to take the place of wood lath, $206.00 extra.
Fire-Chief Shingle Roll Roofing, Red or Sea Green in color, instead of wood shingles, $67.00 less.
Storm Doors and Windows, $59.19 extra.
Screen Doors and Windows, black wire, $31.77 extra; galvanized wire, $36.54 extra.

This house can be built on a lot 45 feet wide.
If ESTIMATES and SPECIFICATIONS for plumbing, hot water, steam or warm air heating systems, electric wiring material, gas or electric fixtures are desired, write for them, mentioning the Clyde Modern Home No. 3033 in your request.

Built at Avon, S. Dak., Oregon, Ill., Canton, Mo., Long Island City, N. Y., Crafton, Neb., Dixon, Iowa, and other cities.

Our Guarantee Protects You—Order Your House From This Book
Price Includes Plans and Specifications

SEARS, ROEBUCK AND CO. CHICAGO

This Clyde has an unusual feature for a house in the middle of an Illinois cornfield: a widow's walk (perched atop the hip roof). When I asked a local resident its purpose, she replied, "That way, the woman of the house could look out over the large cornfield and see if her man was headed home." (Westfield)

This trailing-edge Victorian was a popular house for Sears, remaining in its catalogs until 1920. Despite the vinyl siding and replacement windows, this Sears Clyde retains much of its original charm. (Alton)

TRAILING-EDGE VICTORIAN

TRAILING-EDGE VICTORIAN

$943.00

See Description of Honor Bilt Houses on P...

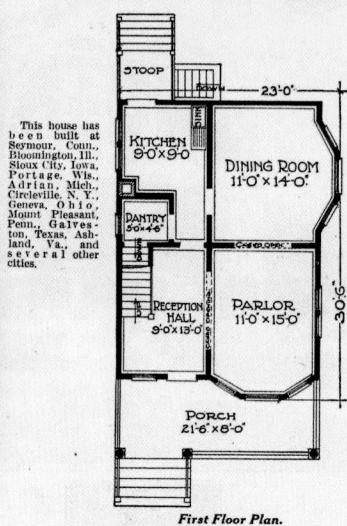

This house has been built at Seymour, Conn., Bloomington, Ill., Sioux City, Iowa, Portage, Wis., Adrian, Mich., Circleville, N.Y., Geneva, Ohio, Mount Pleasant, Penn., Galveston, Texas, Ashland, Va., and several other cities.

First Floor Plan.

Second Floor Plan.

Honor Bilt Modern Home
- No. C2017 "Already Cut" and Fitted. Price, $999.00
- No. C167 Not Cut and Fitted. Price, 943.00

For $943.00 we will furnish all the material to build this Seven-Room House, consisting of Mill Work, Flooring, Ceiling, Siding, Finishing Lumber, Building Paper, Pipe, Gutter, Sash Weights, Hardware, Painting Material, Lumber, Lath and Shingles. NO EXTRAS, as we guarantee enough material at the above price to build this house according to our plans.

Can be furnished 2 feet wider for $45.00 extra.

Price does not include cement, brick or plaster.

First story inside floors, trim, doors, etc., furnished in clear red oak for $67.00 extra.

For Our Offer of Free Plans See Page 6.

THIS is a well proportioned house which affords a great deal of room at a low cost. It is very popular in all sections of the country. Our price for all of the material required in its construction will enable you to make a substantial saving.

First Floor.

A bevel plate glass front door, 3x7 feet, opens from the porch into the reception hall. In this hall there is an open yellow pine stairway leading to the second floor. A cased opening leads from the hall into the parlor and another cased opening from the parlor into the dining room. The kitchen has a good size pantry adjoining it. Please note that we furnish colored leaded art glass sash for the hall. We also furnish a crystal leaded front window for the parlor. Interior doors are made of clear yellow pine with clear grade yellow pine trim, such as casing, baseboard and molding. Inside cellar stairs directly under the main stairs lead to the basement.

Second Floor.

All doors, floors and trim on this floor are of clear yellow pine. The three bedrooms and bathroom can be entered direct from the hall, and all rooms have an abundance of light and air.

Painted two coats outside; color to suit. Varnish and wood filler for two coats of interior finish. Built on a concrete block foundation; No. 1 yellow pine framing lumber; sided with clear cypress narrow bevel siding and has a cedar shingle roof.

Excavated basement under the entire house, 7 feet from floor to joists, with concrete floor. First floor, 9 feet from floor to ceiling; second floor, 8 feet from floor to ceiling.

No. C2017 is furnished with ceiling on second floor, 8 feet 3 inches high from floor.

This house can be built on a lot 30 feet wide.

If estimates and specifications for plumbing, hot water, steam or warm air heating systems are desired write for them, mentioning Modern Home No. C167 or No. C2017 in your request.

Saved $300.00 to $400.00.
Pauling, N. Y.

Sears, Roebuck and Co.,
Chicago, Ill.

Gentlemen:—I am now living in my new home built from your plan No. C167 and I can safely say that by buying all of the material from you to complete this house, I have saved between $300.00 and $400.00. I cheerfully recommend your fair dealings and good quality of goods. Everything is O. K. in every respect. Thanking Sears, Roebuck and Co., I am, Yours truly,
GEORGE H. SLOCUM.

SEARS, ROEBUCK AND CO., CHICAGO, ILLINOIS

—42—

Years ago, this Sears Maytown was used by college students as a frat house. Fortunately, it lived to tell the tale. Today, it still has its original siding and windows. One of its most interesting features is the cantilevered turret on the second floor. (Edwardsville)

Neo-Tudor

Also known as the Tudor Revival, the Neo-Tudor is reminiscent of the English cottage style, first popularized in sixteenth-century England. This housing type is characterized by a cross-gabled, steeply pitched roof, tall, thin windows and dramatic chimneys (often on the home's front). Sears Neo-Tudors were immensely popular because of their practical floor plans, abundant windows, expandable attics, affordable prices and stylish exteriors. The Sears homes featured in this section were some of Sears's bestsellers.

THE DOVER
SIX ROOMS, BATH AND LAVATORY

MODERN HOME No. 3262 ALREADY CUT AND FITTED

THERE is a certain warmth and "hominess" about a wooden house—a readiness to receive the stamp of its owner's personality and an ability to adapt itself to its environment. It answers the needs of well-to-do or modest builder and holds its own in town or country.

The Dover is an Americanized English type Colonial story and a half cottage with a convenient floor plan. The massive chimney helps to "tie in" the front gable and the cowled roof lines help to give a compact appearance. The exterior walls are planned for clear bevel siding but will look equally attractive if shingles are used. In either case, we suggest light colors of paint or stain, in contrast to dark shutters, chimney and weathered roof.

The shutters on the front windows are batten type, to match the batten type circle head front door.

Our home building service will furnish every detail to help you have a home as attractive as the Dover. We guarantee quality and quantity, and our ready cut system of construction conserves your building dollars.

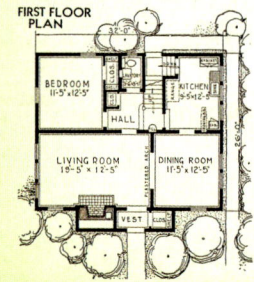

THE FLOOR PLANS

From the terrace, the front door opens into a vestibule which has a large coat closet for outer wraps. Handy for your guests. The living room and dining room extend across the entire front of the house and are connected with a plaster arch, also used from living room to vestibule and hall. Plenty of windows assure bright cheerful rooms and a pleasant outlook.

Most every family can use a first floor bedroom—if not for the family, a guest likes a little privacy from the Master bedrooms. Many have converted this room into a combination library and den and still have a "spare" bedroom available by putting a "rollaway" bed in the closet. Note that the semi-open stairs also open into the kitchen—a step-saving convenience. The kitchen will accommodate cabinets quoted in options. The second floor contains two large bedrooms and the bath is above the average size. Linen storage and good closets. Fill out blank for complete delivered price.

Sears, Roebuck and Co.

I'm looking over a clipped-gable Dover that I overlooked before…The distinguishing features on this Dover are the oversized clipped gables, the bellcast foyer roof that almost kisses the ground and the massive brick chimney. Note the arrangement (and number) of its many windows. (Alton)

Neo-Tudor

The Barrington was a popular model for Sears, but this was also a very popular housing style. Gordon Van Tine (a competing company) also offered a kit home design (the Diana) that was indistinguishable from the Sears Barrington. (Elgin)

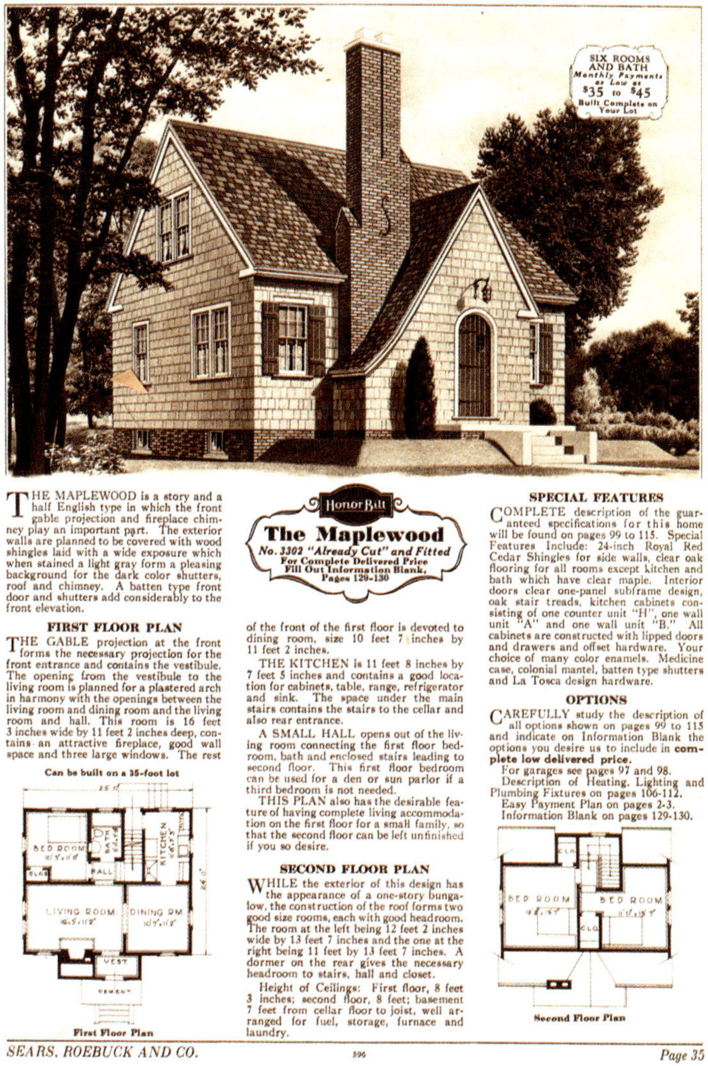

This little Cape Cod is a Maplewood. It's a diminutive version of the Sears Dover, sans clipped gables. (Elgin)

Neo-Tudor

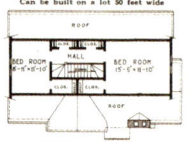

Neo-Tudor

The Lewiston seen at top right is vacant, and judging by its paint job and mildewed masonry, it's been many a year since the lights were on in this solid old house. (Pinckneyville)

The Neo-Tudor shown above was a very popular house for Sears. This Lewiston originally had leaded-glass casement windows beside the fireplace, but as with this house in Dowell, those drafty casements are the first windows to be replaced.

Hundreds of aspiring homeowners selected the Sears Mitchell for their housing needs. Here's a perfect example of the Mitchell in Elgin. While it is a good little house, the roof behind that tall fireplace is often the site of persistent leaks. *Courtesy of Rebecca Hunter.*

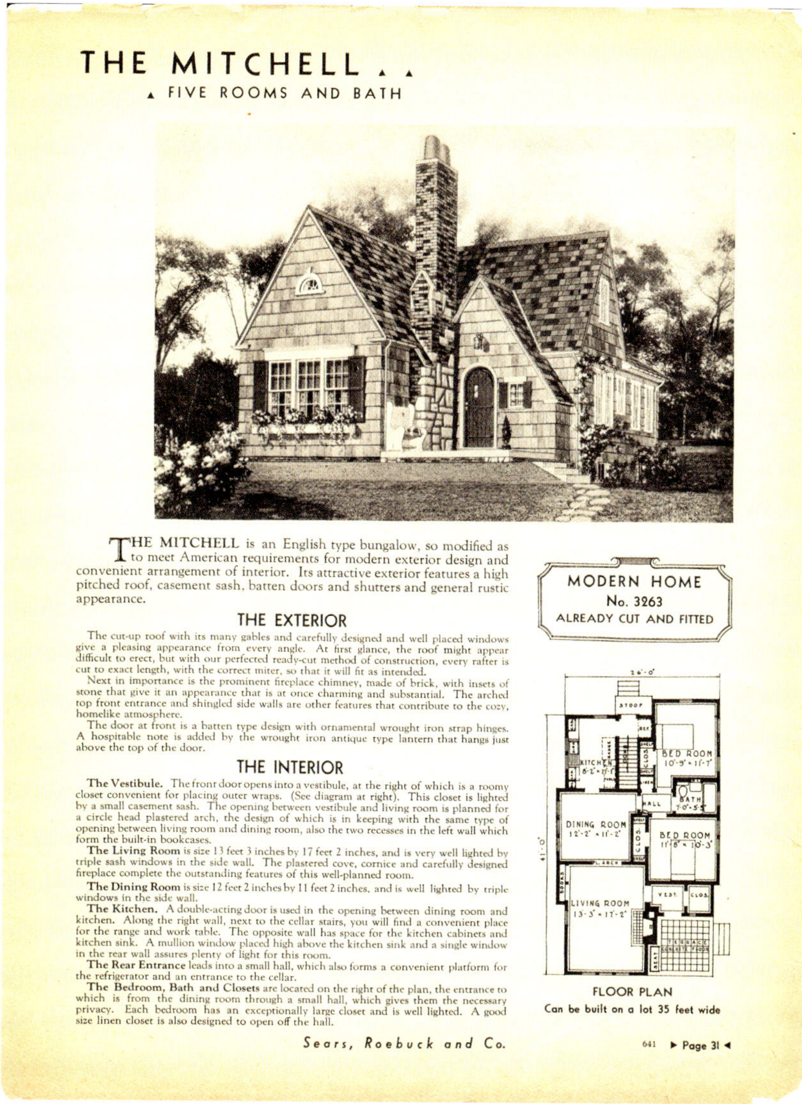

THE MITCHELL
FIVE ROOMS AND BATH

THE MITCHELL is an English type bungalow, so modified as to meet American requirements for modern exterior design and convenient arrangement of interior. Its attractive exterior features a high pitched roof, casement sash, batten doors and shutters and general rustic appearance.

MODERN HOME No. 3263 ALREADY CUT AND FITTED

THE EXTERIOR

The cut-up roof with its many gables and carefully designed and well placed windows give a pleasing appearance from every angle. At first glance, the roof might appear difficult to erect, but with our perfected ready-cut method of construction, every rafter is cut to exact length, with the correct miter, so that it will fit as intended.

Next in importance is the prominent fireplace chimney, made of brick, with insets of stone that give it an appearance that is at once charming and substantial. The arched top front entrance and shingled side walls are other features that contribute to the cozy, homelike atmosphere.

The door at front is a batten type design with ornamental wrought iron strap hinges. A hospitable note is added by the wrought iron antique type lantern that hangs just above the top of the door.

THE INTERIOR

The Vestibule. The front door opens into a vestibule, at the right of which is a roomy closet convenient for placing outer wraps. (See diagram at right). This closet is lighted by a small casement sash. The opening between vestibule and living room is planned for a circle head plastered arch, the design of which is in keeping with the same type of opening between living room and dining room, also the two recesses in the left wall which form the built-in bookcases.

The Living Room is size 13 feet 3 inches by 17 feet 2 inches, and is very well lighted by triple sash windows in the side wall. The plastered cove, cornice and carefully designed fireplace complete the outstanding features of this well-planned room.

The Dining Room is size 12 feet 2 inches by 11 feet 2 inches, and is well lighted by triple windows in the side wall.

The Kitchen. A double-acting door is used in the opening between dining room and kitchen. Along the right wall, next to the cellar stairs, you will find a convenient place for the range and work table. The opposite wall has space for the kitchen cabinets and kitchen sink. A mullion window placed high above the kitchen sink and a single window in the rear wall assures plenty of light for this room.

The Rear Entrance leads into a small hall, which also forms a convenient platform for the refrigerator and an entrance to the cellar.

The Bedroom, Bath and Closets are located on the right of the plan, the entrance to which is from the dining room through a small hall, which gives them the necessary privacy. Each bedroom has an exceptionally large closet and is well lighted. A good size linen closet is also designed to open off the hall.

Sears, Roebuck and Co.

FLOOR PLAN
Can be built on a lot 35 feet wide

Neo-Tudor

NEO-TUDOR

FOUR ROOMS AND BATH
Monthly Payments as Low as $25 to $35
Built Complete on Your Lot

The Rochelle
No. 3282 "Already Cut" and Fitted
For Complete Delivered Price Fill Out Information Blank
Pages 129-130

Can be built on a 40-foot lot

THE FIRST thing you must consider in selecting a home is the size of the house. Too large a home means a waste in investment, unnecessary work and expense and maintenance, and it costs more to furnish a larger house than it does a smaller one. However, by careful planning, it is possible to obtain an efficient, practical arrangement in a small design, which naturally means low cost. Three of the important items you must consider in the cost of a home are excavating, foundation and roof. In studying the Rochelle design you will note that the size of the floor plan is 30 feet wide and 22 feet deep. By eliminating all waste space we have obtained four very practical rooms.

The builder of a small home is also desirous of having the exterior most modern and attractive. Americanized English architecture has been well expressed in the lines of this home. Good window arrangement with shutters, solid white pine batten front door and wood shingles for siding are few of the many noticeable exterior details. Every item of material that enters into the construction of this home is of the same high quality as is furnished in our larger types. The same proportion of saving is created by the fact that all the framework is cut to the exact size, length and thickness at our factory.

FLOOR PLAN
THE PROJECTION which is centered in the front elevation of this home forms a very desirable vestibule, which is also to be intended for use as storage for outer wraps, etc. From the vestibule you pass through an attractive plastered arch into the living room, which is 18 feet 5 inches wide by 11 feet 8 inches deep. This room is also intended to serve as a dining room. The wall space next to the kitchen will be very practical for a drop-leaf dining room table. The room is lighted by three windows, a single window in the front wall and a double sliding window in the side wall, making it light and cheerful.

KITCHEN. The balance of the front of the plan is devoted to the kitchen, where you will note we have indicated a convenient place for all necessary equipment to make it efficient. The entrance to the cellar is from the grade landing with steps leading up to the rear kitchen door. In this space we have also provided a platform for refrigerator storage. The chimney is centrally located so that it can be used for both heating plant and range.

BEDROOMS AND BATH. The arrangement of the bedrooms at the rear of the design gives them the necessary privacy from the street. The left bedroom is size 10 feet 8 inches wide by 9 feet 2 inches deep and has a good size closet in the space next to the bathroom. The opening from the living room into the small hall which connects the right bedroom and bath, is formed by the use of an attractive plastered arch. The right bedroom is larger than the one at the left, being 10 feet 11 inches wide by 9 feet 2 inches deep. The closet for this room is located in the space next to the cellar stairs. The bathroom fixtures which may be installed are as illustrated by our specification No. 22, and we also furnish an attractive built-in medicine case to be placed in the wall above the lavatory.

BASEMENT. The basement is planned to be excavated under the entire building with the exception of the vestibule, and you will find ample room for heating plant, fuel, storage, laundry and fruit room. Height of ceiling from cellar floor to first floor joists is 7 feet.
Height of ceiling of the main rooms is 9 feet from finish floor to plaster.

SPECIAL FEATURES
COMPLETE description of the guaranteed specifications for this home will be found on pages 99 to 115. Special Features Include: 16-inch red cedar shingles for side walls, clear oak flooring for living room; kitchen and bath have clear maple, balance of house clear pine. Interior doors clear one-panel subframe design. Wood medicine case, batten type shutters, and Shefton design hardware.

OPTIONS
CAREFULLY study the description of all options shown on pages 99 to 115 and indicate on Information Blank the options you desire us to include in complete low delivered price.

For Garages see pages 97 and 98.
For description of Heating, Lighting and Plumbing Fixtures see pages 106 to 112.
For Easy Payment Plan see pages 2 and 3.
Information Blank on pages 129 and 130.

SEARS, ROEBUCK AND CO.   596   Page 63

The distinctive Neo-Tudor look of this 1930s Rochelle in Holland was probably stripped away in the 1970s when the aluminum siding was added. Siding installers are hard on old houses and their architectural details. *Courtesy of Rebecca Hunter.*

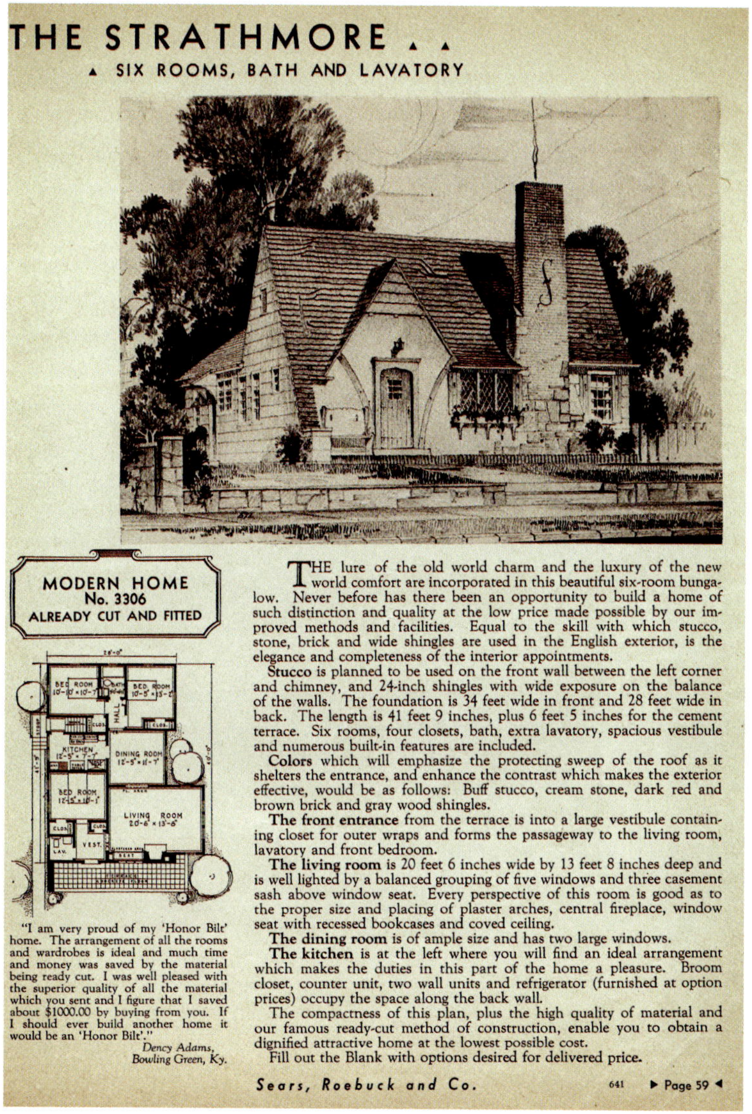

Clad in brick, this house was known as the Hillsboro, and when dressed up in wood siding, it was called the Strathmore. An interesting feature on the Hillsboro/Strathmore is the three casement windows with diamond muntins. (Champaign)

Neo-Tudor

Neo-Tudor

THE NORMANDY
FIVE OR SIX ROOMS, BATH AND RECREATION ROOM

MODERN HOME No. 3390
ALREADY CUT AND FITTED
PRICE $1712.00

THIS attractive French or Normandy type house is another good example of a flexible plan, giving the maximum livable area at the lowest cost consistent with good construction. Distinguished by a beautifully designed turret, capped with antique weathervane and supported by half timber and stucco pediment, forming an interesting circular shaped vestibule.

The exterior walls as shown in photograph, are planned for brick (not included in base price). We recommend using common brick painted white for best appearance. Stained shingles or wood siding can be used with equally pleasing results and at considerable saving in cost.

THE FLOOR PLANS

The newest and one of the most popular ideas being used for both city and suburban homes is the "stepped-up" floor plan. By studying the floor plans, you will note four levels. First—Excavated portion containing game room, laundry and heater room. Second—Regular floor level with living room, dining room and kitchen. Third—Two bedrooms and bath and Fourth—If you desire to finish a third bedroom, a half flight of stairs carries you to the space over the living room.

The economical feature of this home is that you have to excavate only for a depth of 3 ft. (average excavation is 5 ft.) for the left wing only. This entire area can be planned for basement, if desired as the front part provides recreation room or attached motor room. Some have used this space for maid's room and lavatory.

Note the large "L" shaped room elevated to living room and dining room. A pair of French doors in the back wall of dining room open on to the terrace. Kitchen is planned to receive all equipment necessary for step saving work center.

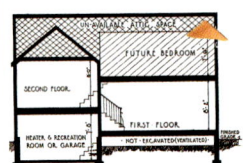

WHAT PRICE INCLUDES

At the price quoted, we guarantee to furnish all the material for this home consisting of lumber, lath, millwork, flooring, shingles, building paper, hardware, metal and paint material according to general specifications shown on pages 8, 9, 10 and 11.

Study introductory pages of this book and select the options which are carefully explained and priced for your convenience. Buy your home from *Sears* and become a happy satisfied home builder.

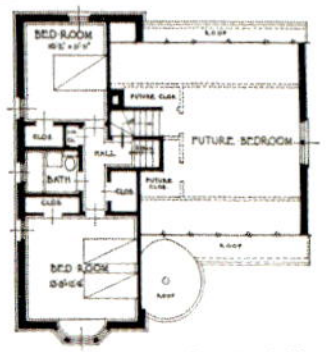

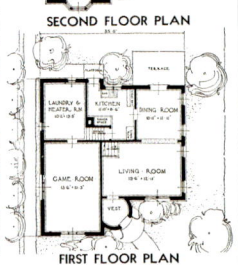

Sears, Roebuck and Co.   642   ▶ Page 23 ◀

This housing style (with the rounded entry foyer) was known as the Normandy, so to keep things simple, Sears named its tri-level version of this house the "Normandy." (Elmhurst)

94

This pretty little Wilmore was one of Sears's most popular Neo-Tudors. Despite the aluminum siding, this house in Mendota is in beautiful condition and looks true to its original catalog picture. *Courtesy of Rebecca Hunter.*

THE WILMORE..
▲ FIVE ROOMS AND BATH

MODERN HOME No. 3327 ALREADY CUT AND FITTED

A FIVE-ROOM bungalow type design. One of the most popular of all American houses. In presenting this economical home, the Wilmore, we not only offer a compact plan of which every foot of floor space has been used to the best advantage, but have also worked out an attractive exterior along the lines commonly known as "Americanized English." The exterior walls of this home are planned to be covered with clear Red Cedar 24-inch shingles, laid with ten-inch exposure. The walls are relieved of any suggestion of plainness by the careful grouping of large well balanced windows, circle head batten type front door with batten type shutters to match.

The specifications include one dip coat and one brush coat of Super quality shingle stain and we suggest using a light gray color with ivory or white trim, and dark brown or green for shutters and front door. All exterior moldings, trim and casings are of clear Cypress, the "Wood Eternal," to be covered with three coats of Sears Master Mixed paint.

This type home requires many pieces of material cut to special miter and detail. This work is all accurately handled in our factory by special machinery and saves you hundreds of dollars in constructing your home.

THE FLOOR PLAN

The entrance over the front terrace is into the vestibule which gives the desired protection and also furnishes a convenient place for hanging outer wraps.

The living room is 15 ft. 2 in. by 12 ft. 5 in., is well lighted by three large windows in the front and side walls. A large front gable covers the projection of the dining room located at the left and connected with the living room by a large plastered arch opening.

The kitchen is sure to make friends among housewives for it has a compact practical arrangement for range, table, refrigerator, sink and cabinets. Cross ventilation is another feature which will be appreciated.

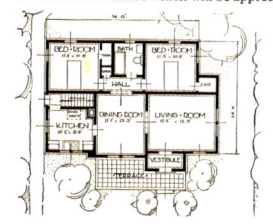

Two well balanced bedrooms with large closets, and with bathroom between, make up the balance of the first floor plan. A small hall gives the necessary privacy to this part of the house and contains a closet for linen.

For slight additional cost we can furnish attic stairway with entrance from dining room.

The size of the Wilmore home is 38 ft. wide and 24 ft. deep and can be built on a 45-foot lot. Height of ceilings 8 ft. 3 in. with 7-ft. basement planned to be excavated under the entire building and to contain furnace, laundry, fruit and fuel storage and plenty of space for recreation room, if desired.

Fill out the blank you will find in the back of this book for complete delivered price, copy of architectural perspective and floor plan, together with outline of specifications.

Sears, Roebuck and Co.   641   ▶ Page 21 ◀

Neo-Tudor

95

Colonial Revival

Early twentieth-century Colonials are not true Colonials because they were not built during the Colonial period (seventeenth- and eighteenth-century America). The proper term is "Colonial Revival" because they are a revival of that popular housing style. The classic Colonial Revival is the Sears Lexington, a perfectly symmetrical two-story house with five front windows, a small front porch, tall brick chimneys on either end and a center hallway (with centered front door). When advertisers want to depict a happy home as a backdrop for their products, the architectural style featured is often a Colonial Revival. It really is America's favorite house.

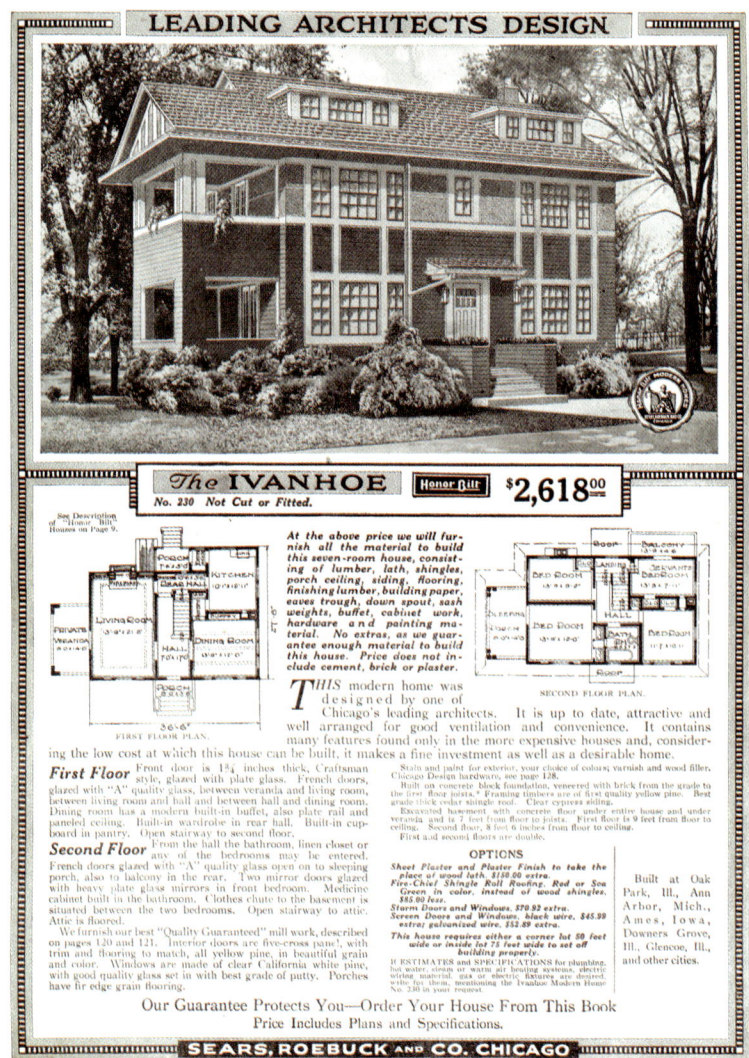

This Ivanhoe in Elmhurst is in excellent condition. The side porches (upper and lower) and the front porch were enclosed, and a second front porch was added to its front, but the changes were thoughtfully done.

Colonial Revival

The Crescent seen above is in Wheaton and is in largely original condition. Note the old wooden windows and their unusual lites. It's rare to find a home of this vintage with its original storm windows still in place.

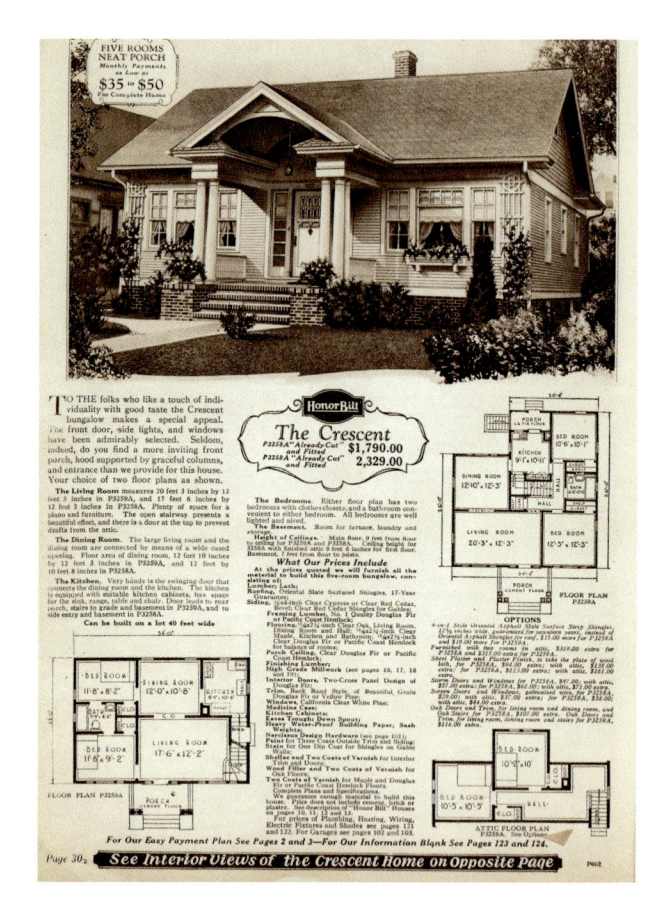

One of Sears's most popular houses, the Crescent was offered in two floor plans, and both offered an expandable attic with space for two extra bedrooms. A distinctive feature of the Crescent is the oversized front porch roof with cornice returns and the little triangle within its peak, as seen at top left. (Glen Ellyn)

Sitting smack dab in a commercially zoned part of Godfrey, this Crescent is still used as a single-family residence. Because of its commercial zoning, and its relatively poor condition, I fear this Crescent's days may be numbered.

The CRESCENT INTERIORS

ABOVE—The Pleasant Dining Room.
BELOW—The Modern Bathroom.

These views show one of many ways to furnish The Crescent Home.

ABOVE—The Living Room looking towards the Dining Room and stairs to second floor.
CENTER—The Stairway to the second floor.
BELOW—The front Bedroom has plenty of light and cross current of air.

ABOVE—The Kitchen is equipped with built-in Cupboards.
BELOW—Just a glimpse of a Bedroom in the attic. See options.

See Description of the Crescent Home on Opposite Page

Colonial Revival

99

THE JEFFERSON
EIGHT ROOMS AND TWO BATHS

THE "JEFFERSON" is designed along the same lines as historic Mount Vernon, and is a true example of Southern Colonial architecture—the same type that has endured in many instances for generation after generation. The Southern Colonial type has held its share of popularity from the beginning. Exterior walls of white-painted brick provide a substantial appearance and form a pleasing background for the dark green shutters and roof.

MODERN HOME No. 3349 NOT ALREADY CUT

THE FLOOR PLAN

Dining Room, Kitchen, Living Room and useful, attractive Sun Room all open off the center hall on the first floor. Note the two convenient closets off the vestibule, for outer wraps.

Second floor plan contains hall, four large roomy bedrooms and two baths. This roomy home boasts a total of eleven closets.

Fill out the Information Blank and we will send you complete delivered price, photographic architectural elevations and floor plans, also outline of specifications.

WHAT OUR PRICE INCLUDES

At the base price quoted, we will furnish all materials needed to build this home, (except brick and masonry) consisting of lumber, lath, roof shingles, building paper, millwork and 6-Panel Doors, Colonial Back Band trim, Kitchen Cabinets, Linoleum for Kitchen, Bath and Lavatory, Oak flooring in remainder of rooms, Elgin Manhattan hardware, enamel for interior trim, varnish for doors and floors, sheet metal and outside paint materials.

Sears, Roebuck and Co.

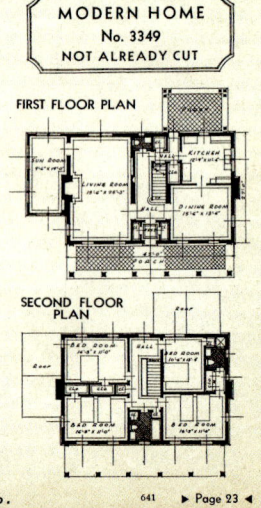

For those who say that Sears homes were small and boxy, here's the counter-argument: the Sears Jefferson. This Jefferson is in Carbondale and is the only one I've ever seen. Thanks to Rebecca Hunter for this find!

The center-hallway Colonial Revival was one of the most popular housing styles of the 1920s and '30s. The Lexington was a classic example of this style. Notice the odd placement of the window and door on the second-floor balcony. (Glen Ellyn)

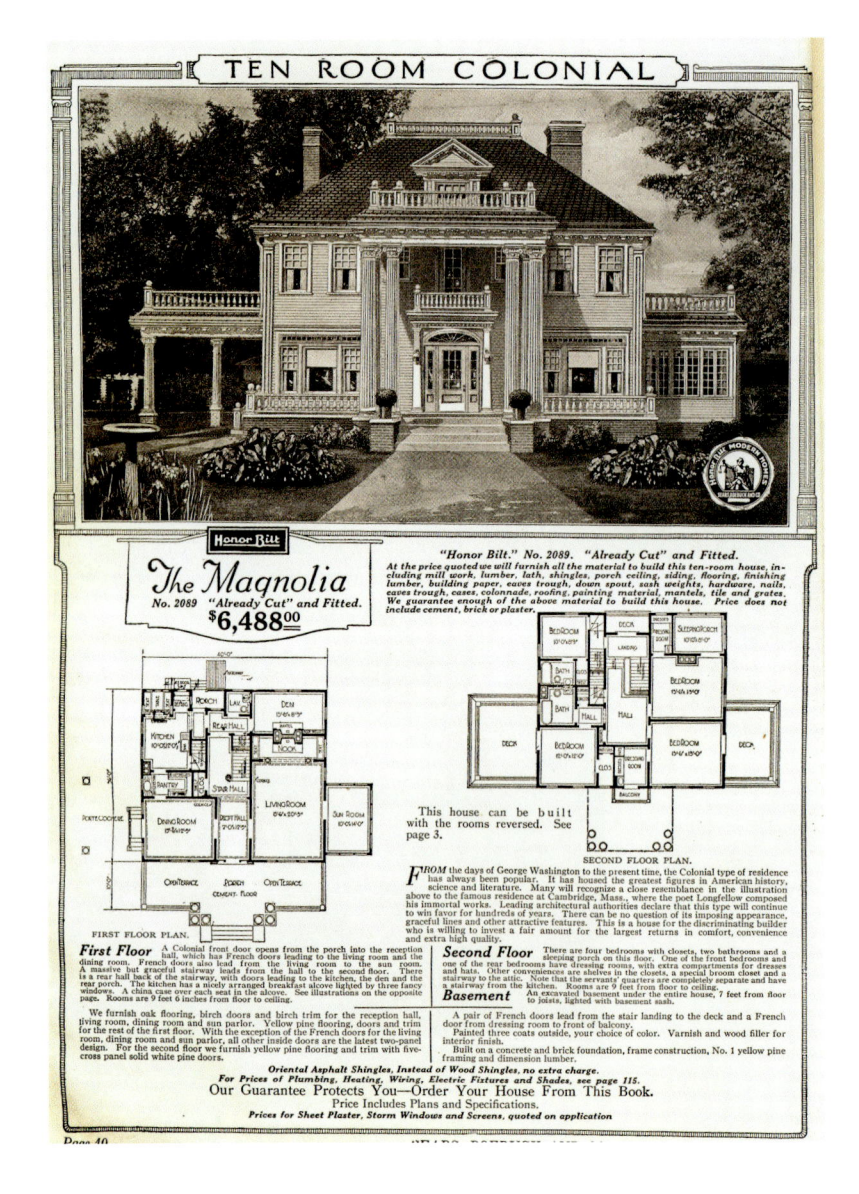

Sears's biggest and best house was the Sears Magnolia. There are no known Magnolias in Illinois, but perhaps there are a few hidden away that have yet to be discovered. This Magnolia is in Benson, North Carolina.

Lovely example of a Madelia on Wood River's Ninth Street. Notice the pent roof extending from the front porch to the side porch. The vinyl-clad starburst in the front gable is not original.

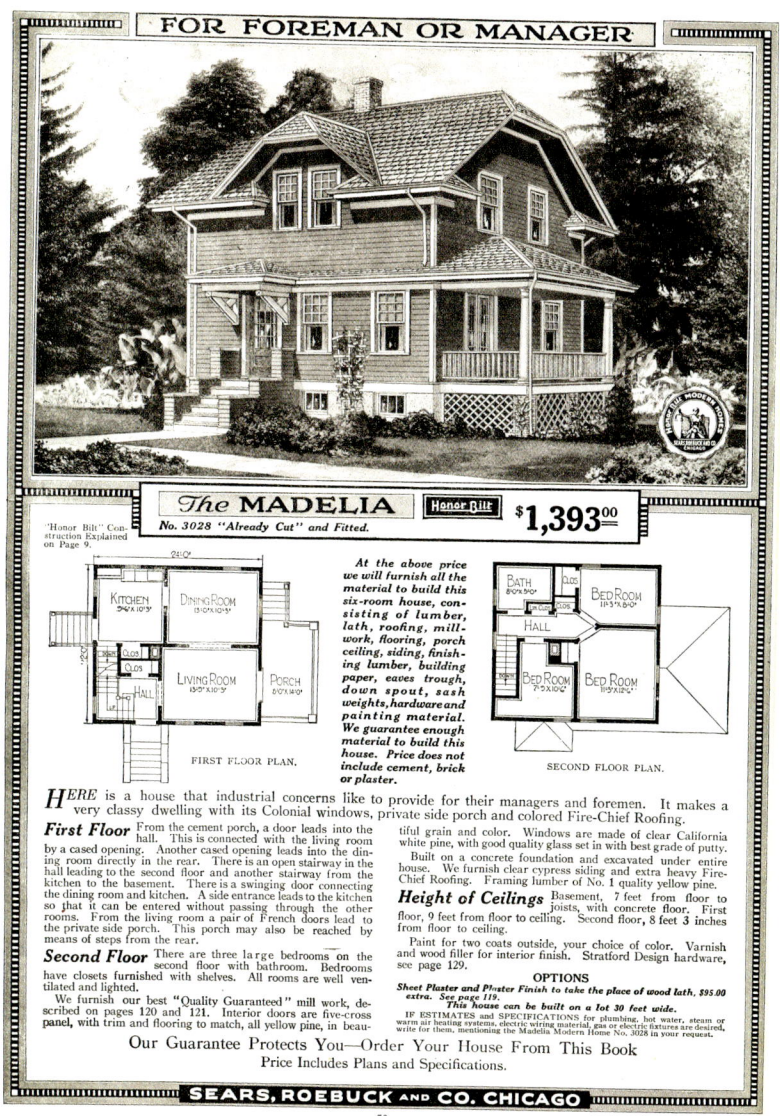

FOR FOREMAN OR MANAGER

The MADELIA — Honor Bilt — $1,393.00
No. 3028 "Already Cut" and Fitted.

At the above price we will furnish all the material to build this six-room house, consisting of lumber, lath, roofing, millwork, flooring, porch ceiling, siding, finishing lumber, building paper, eaves trough, down spout, sash weights, hardware and painting material. We guarantee enough material to build this house. Price does not include cement, brick or plaster.

HERE is a house that industrial concerns like to provide for their managers and foremen. It makes a very classy dwelling with its Colonial windows, private side porch and colored Fire-Chief Roofing.

First Floor From the cement porch, a door leads into the hall. This is connected with the living room by a cased opening. Another cased opening leads into the dining room directly in the rear. There is an open stairway in the hall leading to the second floor and another stairway from the kitchen to the basement. There is a swinging door connecting the dining room and kitchen. A side entrance leads to the kitchen so that it can be entered without passing through the other rooms. From the living room a pair of French doors lead to the private side porch. This porch may also be reached by means of steps from the rear.

Second Floor There are three large bedrooms on the second floor with bathroom. Bedrooms have closets furnished with shelves. All rooms are well ventilated and lighted.

We furnish our best "Quality Guaranteed" mill work, described on pages 120 and 121. Interior doors are five-cross panel, with trim and flooring to match, all yellow pine, in beautiful grain and color. Windows are made of clear California white pine, with good quality glass set in with best grade of putty. Built on a concrete foundation and excavated under entire house. We furnish clear cypress siding and extra heavy Fire-Chief Roofing. Framing lumber of No. 1 quality yellow pine.

Height of Ceilings Basement, 7 feet from floor to joists, with concrete floor. First floor, 9 feet from floor to ceiling. Second floor, 8 feet 3 inches from floor to ceiling.

Paint for two coats outside, your choice of color. Varnish and wood filler for interior finish. Stratford Design hardware, see page 129.

OPTIONS
Sheet Plaster and Plaster Finish to take the place of wood lath, $95.00 extra. See page 119.
This house can be built on a lot 30 feet wide.
IF ESTIMATES and SPECIFICATIONS for plumbing, hot water, steam or warm air heating systems, electric wiring material, gas or electric fixtures are desired, write for them, mentioning the Madelia Modern Home No. 3028 in your request.

Our Guarantee Protects You—Order Your House From This Book
Price Includes Plans and Specifications.

SEARS, ROEBUCK AND CO. CHICAGO

COLONIAL REVIVAL

103

DUTCH COLONIAL

Another very popular housing style is the Dutch Colonial, a close cousin of the Colonial Revival. A key feature of this house is the gambrel (barn-shaped) roof. In America's early years (1600s and 1700s), these houses were built by the Dutch in "New Amsterdam," a little city near the Hudson River. In 1664, New Amsterdam was renamed New York. The popularity of these twentieth-century Dutch Colonials inspired Sears to offer several of its own designs. The Martha Washington and the Puritan were the Papa Bear and Baby Bear versions. This generation of Dutch Colonials was popular from the 1910s to the early 1930s. It's interesting to note that these twentieth-century homes bear little resemblance to the true Dutch Colonials found in New England.

THE NEWBURY..
▲ SIX ROOMS, BATH AND LARGE PORCH

MODERN HOME No. 3397
ALREADY CUT AND FITTED

Dignified in every line and proportion, this aristocratic member of the Colonial period has many prototypes in all parts of the United States. Some of the original homes built by early settlers along the Atlantic seaboard, have stood and served as lovely homes for more than a century—testifying to the permanence of design and good construction.

Inviting indeed, is the large front porch inset under the graceful sweep of the main roof. Well proportioned square columns tie it in as a part of the main structure. Screened in summer, it forms a most popular place.

The dormer shown on the front perspective is repeated on the rear and helps to break up the otherwise large roof areas. The stone base of the chimney is an unusual and interesting detail. The front wall under the porch roof is planned to be covered with brick, while the balance of the walls are of wide bevel siding which we suggest painting white or cream.

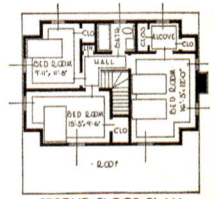

SECOND FLOOR PLAN
If second bathroom is needed, it will work out nicely in alcove and closet space.

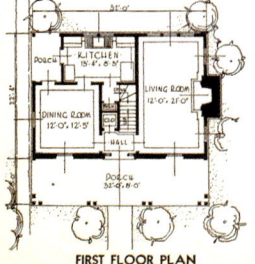

THE FLOOR PLANS

On each side of the six panel Colonial front, door glazed sidelights furnish brightness and necessary light to the central hall where you also have a convenient closet for wraps. Every home builder will enjoy planning and furnishing the large living room with open fireplace. The rear porch is accessible from both dining room and kitchen and gives the necessary protection. The kitchen is a real efficient work center with good light and wall space for all necessary equipment. Cellar stairs and broom closet are located under the main stairs.

The wide enclosed stairway leads to upstairs hall which connects the three bedrooms and bath. The Master bedroom is above the average size with dressing alcove, two closets and three exposures. No waste space in this home. Every foot is used to the best advantage. The location of the bath enables all plumbing fixtures to "plumb in" in one stack.

The plan is 32 ft. wide and 30 ft. 4 in. deep and will look attractive on a lot 50 feet wide.

FIRST FLOOR PLAN

▶ Page 28 ◀   641   *Modern Homes Division*

Notice the base of the chimney on this Newbury. It starts as stone and rises into brick. Also notice the full-width front porch and the gentle swoop of the bellcast roof. (Elmhurst)

DUTCH COLONIAL

A scaled-down version of the Martha Washington, this Puritan has all the classic markings of a Dutch Colonial, right down to the rounded hood over the stoop. (Mound City)

This Martha Washington in Lombard has its original wooden windows and original storms, too. The Dutch Colonial was a common housing style, and the Sears version had few features to differentiate it from other Dutch Colonials. *Courtesy of Rebecca Hunter.*

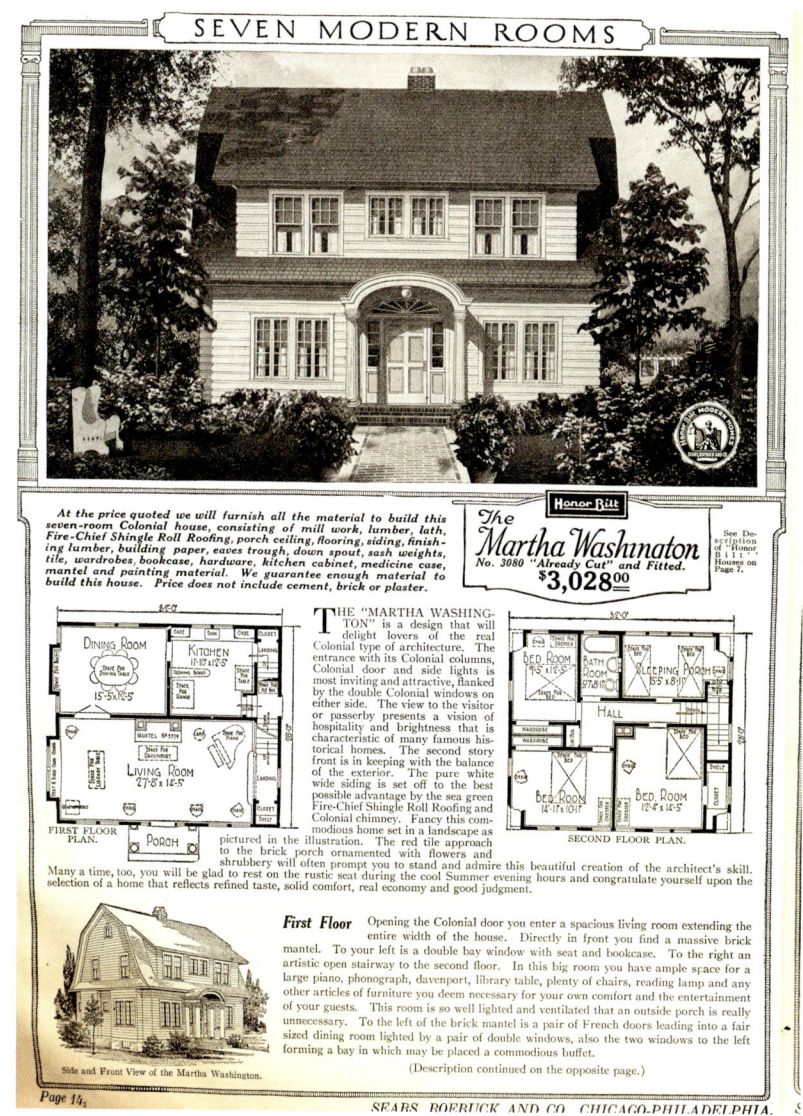

DUTCH COLONIAL

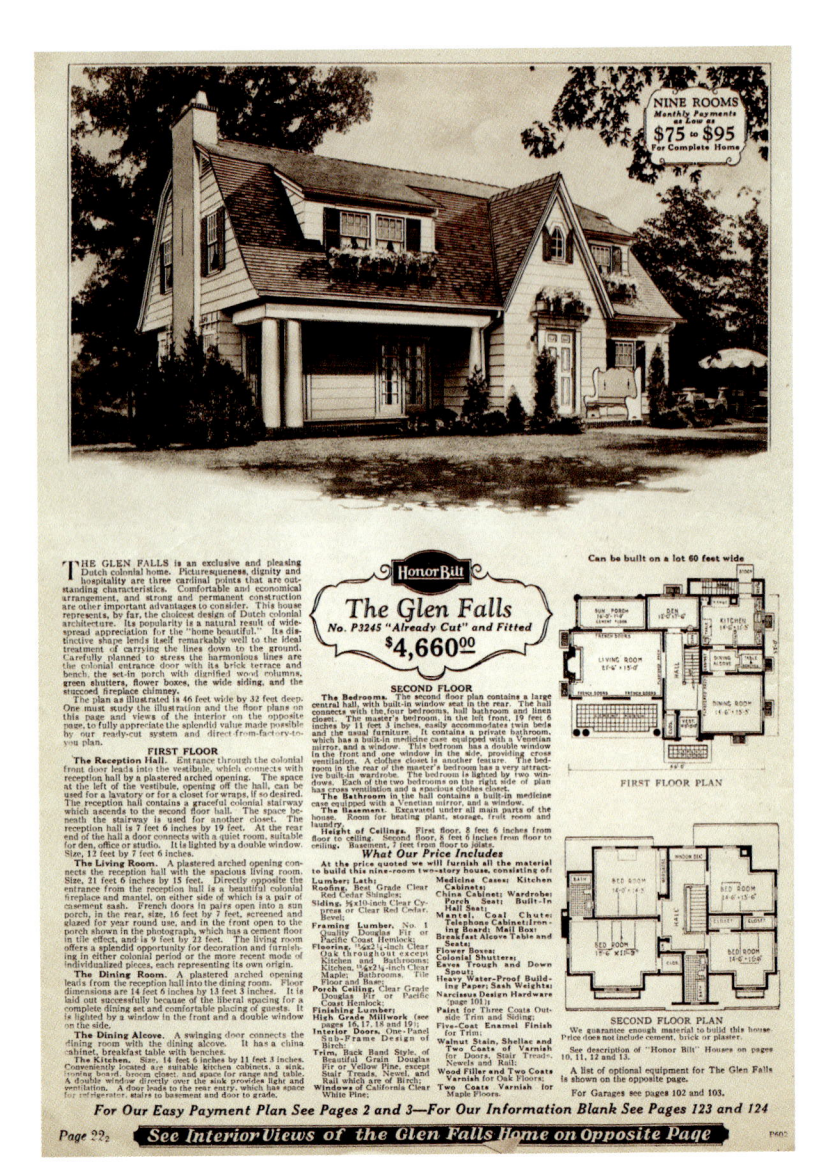

The Glenn Falls was one of Sears's finest homes. Unlike many Glenn Falls that I've seen, this one still has its open porch (on the left). These are frequently enclosed.

A mid-size Dutch Colonial in Barrington, Illinois. This model was the Van Dorn. *Courtesy of Rebecca Hunter.*

Bungalow (One-Story)

The word "bungalow" comes from India (specifically Bengal), where tiny houses with large porches and big eaves were called "banglas." In the first years of the twentieth century, bungalows quickly became America's most popular little house. As people came to understand and accept the newly discovered germ theory, those dust bunny–collecting Victorian manses with their ornate woodwork, fretwork and gingerbread fell from favor with a resounding thud. Salutary simplicity became the keynote for "modern" homebuyers. The distinctive characteristics of a bungalow are oversized eaves supported by brackets, exposed rafter tails, simple design and a low-pitched roof extending over a wide porch. Sears's bungalows were a hit because they were modest, affordable and easy to build—an especially important characteristic for a twelve-thousand-piece kit!

The high arch and dentil molding on the front porch of the Columbine is probably its most distinctive feature. The two-story addition on the right side was nicely done and is in keeping with the home's original design.

BUNGALOW (ONE-STORY)

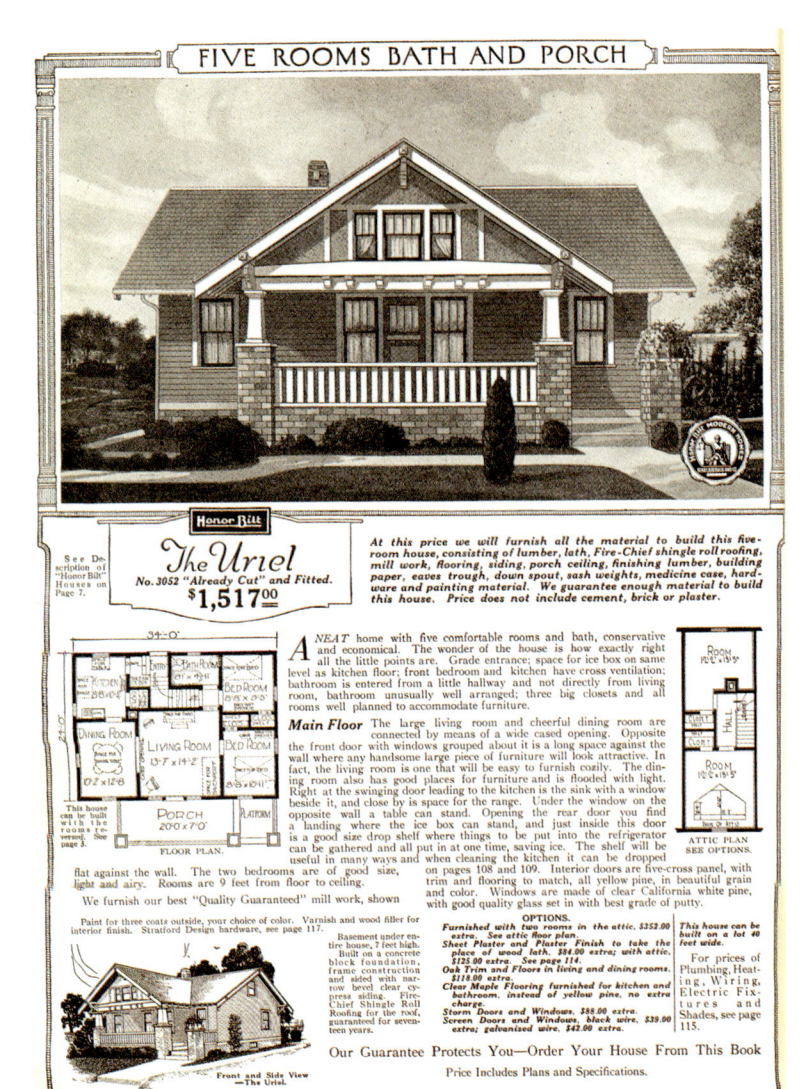

This Uriel (also known as the Conway) in Park Ridge is in beautiful condition. The oversized front porch on this house is frequently converted into living space. *Courtesy of Dale Patrick Wolicki.*

112

The Argyle was one of Sears's most popular homes. Sadly, this little Argyle is the victim of insensitive remodeling, including a crossword puzzle screened porch and a second-floor addition that looks nothing like the existing structure. (Wood River)

BUNGALOW (ONE-STORY)

Bungalow (One-Story)

The Elsmore was one of Sears's top-ten most popular models. This Elsmore in Park Ridge has innumerable original features, such as the porch railing and columns, gable ornament, half-round galvanized gutters and small attic window. *Courtesy of Dale Patrick Wolicki.*

Years ago, I startled my husband when I came running in the back door yelling, "I just saw my first Fairy!" Pictured here is a fine-looking Fairy in Elgin.

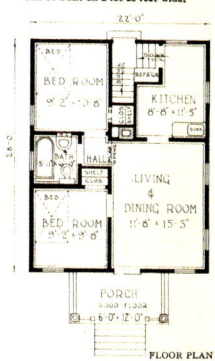

Bungalow (One-Story)

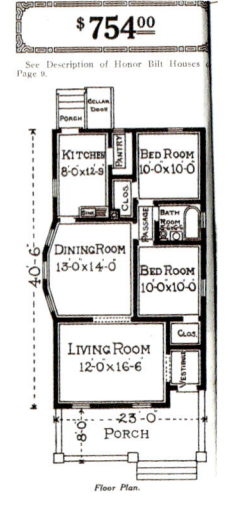

BUNGALOW (ONE-STORY)

The arched porch roof is a distinctive feature on Modern Home #229. The diamond muntins on the front window are also unique, but often the windows in ninety-year-old homes have been replaced. (Metropolis)

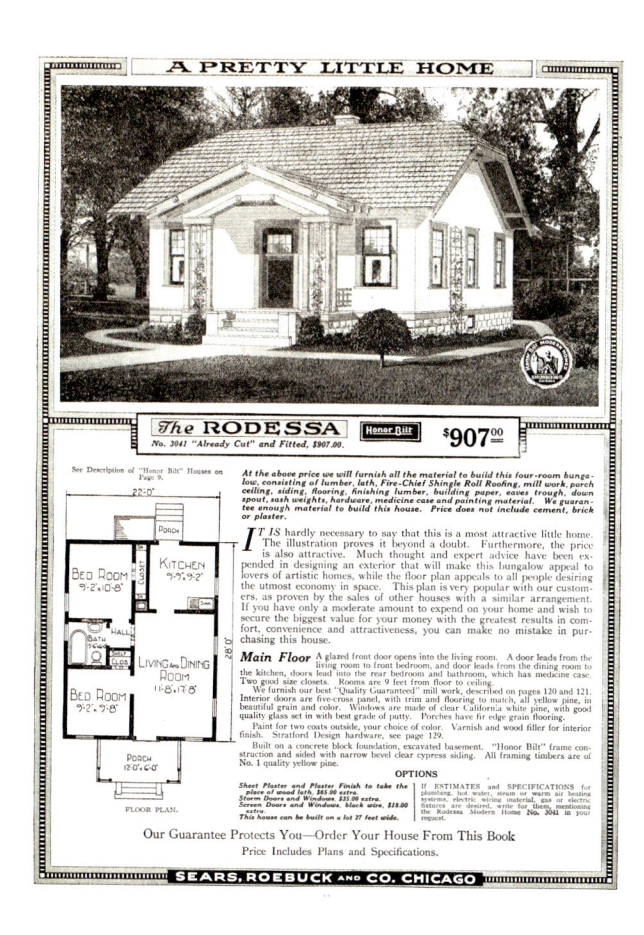

Seen at the top right are the two Rodessas—in the flesh—at the site of the old Sears mill in Cairo. Which one is the pre-cut home? That's a mystery!

Even though the porch was closed in, the little Rodessa seen above still has the distinctive lines of its original porch roof. The bathroom window on the side of the house has also been closed in, which is very common. Many of these early Sears homes had bathtubs but no showers. (Cairo)

Bungalow (One-Story)

Left: Some interior views of the Osborn. Notice the built-in bookcases and wood-accented wainscoting in the dining room. For $148, you could upgrade from pine millwork to oak for the entire living room and dining room.

Below: An Osborn in Mattoon. Notice the matching garage in the backyard.

A beautiful example of a Sears Osborn, built by Henry and Ethel Mohr in 1928.

Bungalow (One-Story)

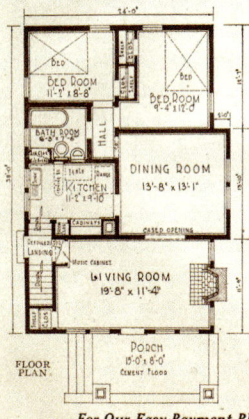

One of the first houses I successfully identified was the Sears Oakdale. The odd placement of the kitchen door (on the home's side but so close to the front) is a key feature that is easy to catch. (Cairo)

120

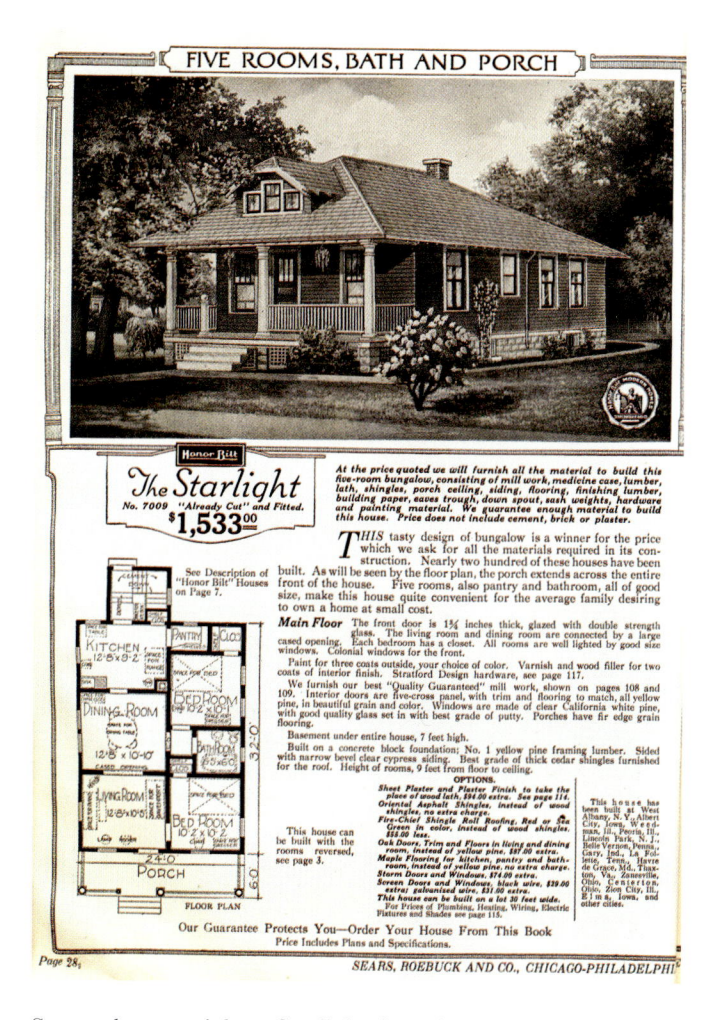

Seen at bottom right, a Starlight sits quietly next to a large, 1950s brick school. This house in Alton is in delightfully original condition.

The Starlight seen at top was one of Sears's most popular designs and was offered with a shed dormer, gabled dormer or (as shown here) a clipped-gable dormer. This house was offered in the Sears catalog from the early 1910s to the late 1930s. (Duquoin)

Bungalow (One-Story)

121

BUNGALOW (ONE-STORY)

ARISTOCRAT OF BUNGALOWS

The ASHMORE — Honor Bilt — $2,870.00
No. 3034 "Already Cut" and Fitted.

At the above price we will furnish all the material to build this six-room bungalow, consisting of mill work, medicine cabinet, buffet, kitchen cupboard, lumber, lath, shingles, porch ceiling, flooring, finishing lumber, building paper, eaves trough, down spout, sash weights, hardware and painting material. No extras, as we guarantee enough material to build this bungalow. Inside floors, trim, doors, etc., furnished in clear red oak for $230.00 extra. Price does not include cement, brick or plaster.

IN THE original conception of this bungalow, brown was made the predominating color. The treatment of the roof, body finish, floors and walls of interior, with a careful blending of tone from the darker brown to light terra cotta and creams, produces a delightful and harmonious contrast. The rugged, massive cobblestone chimney adds the final touch of stability and bungalow character.

Main Floor Front door opens into large living room with a fireplace nook two steps above the floor. At either side of the fireplace are roomy, built-in bookcases with glass doors and sash above. To the right of the living room is a bay window with a comfortable seat built in. The walls of this room are paneled, cove mold in ceiling. A cased opening leads from the living room into the dining room. Here you will find a handsome buffet. From the living room a door opens into the front bedroom. From the dining room a pair of French doors open upon the pergola. In the kitchen will be found the ever popular Pullman breakfast alcove. There is a broad work shelf at one side of the sink with cupboard and bins beneath. Kitchen also has a disappearing ironing board. Two well lighted and well ventilated bedrooms in the rear. From the passageway there is a stairway to the attic which contains space to be finished into other rooms, such as den or storage room. There is a stairway from the kitchen to the basement. A linen closet and clothes chute in hall. Towel closet opens into bathroom. The door in the closet in the bedroom adjoining kitchen has a large mirror on the bedroom side. **Double floors in all rooms.**

Basement Excavated basement, with concrete floor under rear half of the house, well lighted, 7 feet from floor to joists.

Rooms on the main floor are 9 feet high. This bungalow is built on a concrete foundation. No. 1 yellow pine frame construction, sided and roofed with best grade thick red cedar shingles.
We furnish our best "Quality Guaranteed" mill work, described on pages 120 and 121. Interior doors are five-cross panel, with trim and flooring to match, all yellow pine, in beautiful grain and color. Windows are made of clear California white pine, with good quality glass set in with best grade of putty. Front and side porches have cement floors.

OPTIONS
Sheet Plaster and Plaster Finish to take the place of wood lath, $130.00 extra.
Fire-Chief Shingle Roll Roofing. Red or Sea Green in color, instead of wood shingles, $74.00 less.
Storm Doors and Windows, $81.19 extra.
Screen Doors and Windows, black wire, $47.76 extra; galvanized wire, $54.92 extra.
Can be built on a lot 45 feet wide.

Paint for two coats outside; stain for shingled siding; varnish and wood filler for interior finish. Chicago Design hardware, see page 128.

Our Guarantee Protects You—Order Your House From This Book
Price Includes Plans and Specifications.

SEARS, ROEBUCK AND CO. CHICAGO
—88—

INTERIORS — The ASHMORE

The Living Room, Looking From Fireplace Nook
Graceful Panel Work.

The Living Room, Looking Toward Fireplace
Note the Rustic Mantel.

The Dining Room
We Furnish the Built-In Buffet.

The Pullman Breakfast Alcove in Kitchen

THE rustic mantel, the bookcase and the elevated fireplace platform in the living room in this strictly up to date bungalow, as well as the graceful panels, indicate refinement and good taste. It would be difficult in a building of this character to embody more attractive features than we show in the interiors herewith presented. Happy is the man who can call a house like this his own.

There is an appearance of comfort in the dining room. When furnished as shown in the illustration and when lighted in subdued effects, it will present a most cheerful and inviting appearance. The homelike and hospitable suggestions in the exterior treatment are duplicated in every line of the interior.

Long before the "kiddies" are awake, the busy business man is up and around, ready for his eggs and bacon or steaming flapjacks. The Pullman Breakfast Alcove in the kitchen provides a snug retreat where the morning meal can be served. The kitchen range close by makes the labor easy for the lady of the house or maid.

SEARS, ROEBUCK AND CO. CHICAGO
—89—

122

A classic Arts and Crafts bungalow, this Sears Ashmore in Waverly is in wonderfully original condition. From the wooden railings on the front porch to the oversized verge boards on the trim, this Ashmore is a real beauty and a spot-on match to the catalog image. This was my favorite find in Illinois.

BUNGALOW (ONE-STORY)

$1,330.00

Honor Bilt Modern Home No. C124

Built at Texarkana, Ark., Washington, D. C., East Greenwich, R. I., Lombard, Ill., Taylorville, Ill., Grand Rapids, Mich., Brooklyn, N. Y., Dunkirk, N. Y., New York, N. Y., Montvale, N. J., Youngstown, Ohio, and North Crystal Lake, Ill.

First Floor Plan.   *Second Floor Plan.*

For $1,330.00 we will furnish all the material to build this Nine-Room Two-Story Bungalow, consisting of Mill Work, Ceiling, Siding, Flooring, Finishing Lumber, Building Paper, Pipe, Gutter, Sash Weights, Hardware, Painting Material, Mantel, Lumber, Lath and Shingles. NO EXTRAS, as we guarantee enough material at the above price to build this bungalow according to our plans.

Price does not include cement, brick or plaster.

First story inside floors, trim, doors, etc., furnished in clear red oak for $83.00 extra.

For Our Offer of Free Plans See Page 6.

THIS two-story bungalow is fast becoming a great favorite in the Central, Eastern and Western states. It has been built in several cities in Illinois, Michigan, New York, New Jersey, Ohio, Rhode Island and Arkansas, as well as in Washington, D. C. Everyone who has built it is pleased with the fine quality of the materials.

First Floor. A large porch extends across the front of the house. Front door leads from the porch into a large reception hall. Cased openings lead from this reception hall into the living room and dining room. We furnish a brick mantel for the living room. A unique arrangement is the open stairway in the rear of the reception hall. Doors are five-cross panel yellow pine with clear yellow pine trim. The windows are divided into eight and twelve lights. Double floors in all rooms.

Second Floor. This floor has four bedrooms, a large hall and a bathroom. All doors are clear solid five-cross panel yellow pine with clear yellow pine trim to match. Bedrooms have an abundance of light, each room having two windows, one on each side.

Painted two coats outside; your choice of color. Wood filler and varnish for two coats of interior finish.

There is an excavated cellar, 10x14 feet, 7 feet from floor to joists. The rooms on the first floor are 9 feet from floor to ceiling; second floor, 9 feet 6 inches from floor to ceiling. This bungalow is built on a concrete block foundation. No. 1 yellow pine frame construction, sided with narrow bevel clear cypress siding over good sheathing and has cedar shingle roof.

This bungalow can be built on a lot 50 feet wide.

If estimates and specifications for plumbing, hot water, steam or warm air heating systems are desired write for them, mentioning Modern Home No. C124 in your request.

—76—

This Modern Home #124 retains many of its original features, including wood siding, clapboard columns and its diamond attic vent. (Crystal Lake)

124

Dressed up in pretty yellow cypress siding, this Sears Walton in Glen Ellyn looks like it stepped off the pages of the Sears Modern Homes catalog. Notice the oversized front porch and how its roofline is angled differently from the primary roof.

BUNGALOW (ONE-STORY)

Bungalow
(One-and-a-Half-Story)

These bungalows featured a gable or shed dormer on the second floor, creating extra space and ventilation for additional bedrooms. Often these dormered bungalows are called "Craftsman-style bungalows." Many people mistakenly confuse this name with a line of tools that Sears offered—known as Craftsman tools—reasoning (erroneously) that all Craftsman-style bungalows are Sears homes. Not true! Sears's well-known tools share no common history with these dormered bungalows.

The Modern Homes catalog promised that the Belmont was both "practical and graceful," and this little Belmont in Mattoon lives up to that promise. The home's exterior retains many of its original features, including windows (and original wooden storms), wood siding, five-piece eave brackets and a small covered stoop at the back of the house.

Bungalow (One-and-a-Half-Story)

The wooden clapboards that originally clothed the little Carlin seen at bottom right have been replaced with cedar planks and brick veneer. The replacement windows, crossbuck aluminum door and modern decking on the front porch are also inappropriate for this early twentieth-century bungalow. (Wood River)

Other than being draped in yellow vinyl siding, the Carlin seen at top still looks much like it did when built in 1919. Note how the rear roofline does not extend down as far as the front roofline. This is a distinctive feature of the Carlin. (Wood River)

Perfect little Sears Savoy in Marshall (on the Illinois/Indiana border). The two pairs of French doors are still intact, as is the porte cochere.

Bungalow (One-and-a-Half-Story)

BUNGALOW (ONE-AND-A-HALF-STORY)

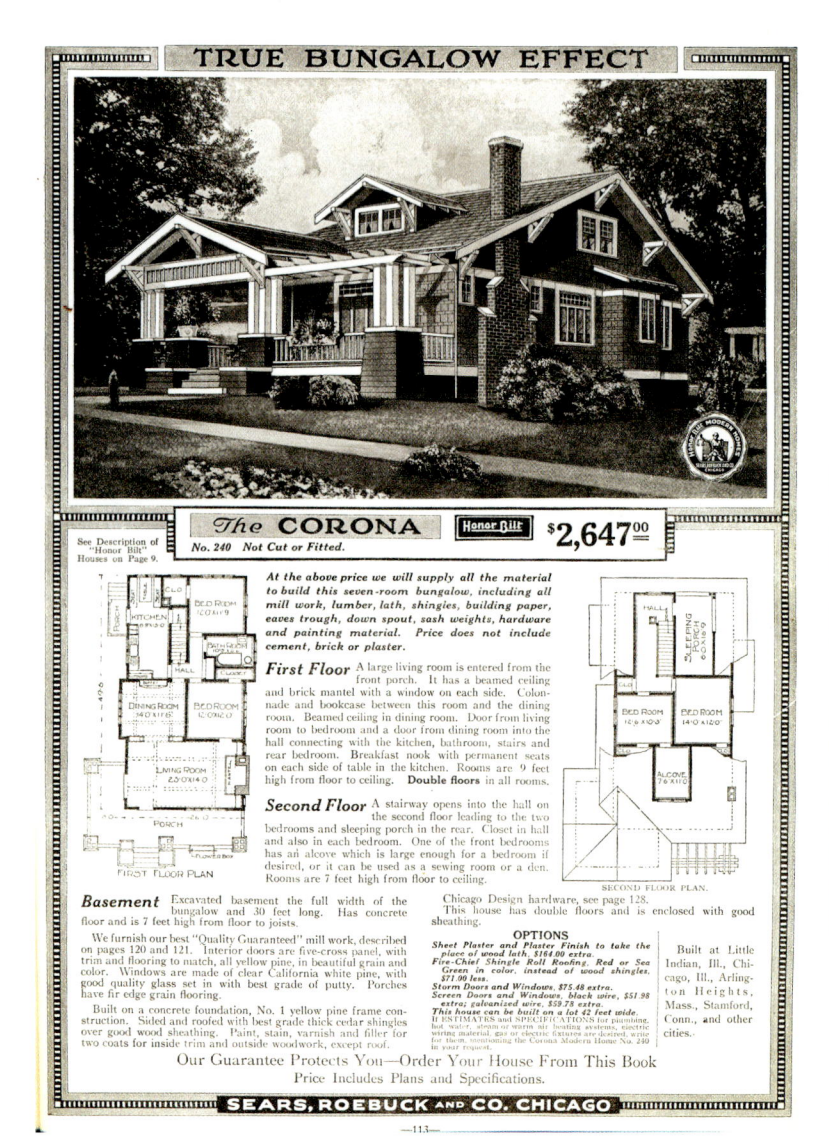

The Arts and Crafts styling on this Corona is both dramatic and beautiful. Even the original front porch pergola remains. A distinctive feature of this Corona is the oversized front porch and the dormer window centered on the roofline. (Gillespie)

Set in the lush rolling hills of Pulaski County, this Bandon probably looks much like it did when first built in 1921, even down to the ornamental design on the fireplace chimney. This is the only example of the Sears Bandon that I've seen in my many travels.

BUNGALOW (ONE-AND-A-HALF-STORY)

This house has been built at Clinton, Ill., Indianapolis, Ind., Salem, Ohio, Gary, Ind., Bloomington, Ill., Plymouth, Ind., Griggsville, Ill., Middleton, Ohio, and other cities.

$1,126.00

See Description of Honor Bilt Houses on Page 9.

Honor Bilt MODERN HOME
No. C2025 "Already Cut" and Fitted. Price, $1,189.00
No. C172 Not Cut and Fitted. Price, 1,126.00

For $1,126.00 we will furnish all the material to build this Five-Room Bungalow, consisting of Lumber, Lath, Shingles, Mill Work, Flooring, Ceiling, Siding, Sideboard, Finishing Lumber, Building Paper, Pipe, Gutter, Sash Weights, Hardware and Painting Material. NO EXTRAS, as we guarantee enough material at the above price to build this house according to our plans.

Price does not include cement, brick or plaster.
Inside floors, trim, doors, etc., furnished in clear red oak for $95.00 extra.

For Our Offer of Free Plans See Page 6.

A MODERN bungalow of frame construction. Extra wide siding (or shingles if preferred), the visible rafters over porches and eaves give a pleasing rustic effect. The roof is ornamented by an attractive dormer with three sash. The front and side of the bungalow are beautified by triple and double windows, making every room light and airy. The porch extends across the front of the house and is 29 feet 6 inches wide by 9 feet 6 inches deep, making a cool and shady retreat. Porch columns are arranged in clusters, supported by a base which is sided with clear cypress bungalow siding. Can be furnished with cedar shingle siding as shown in illustration for the same price.

Floor Plan.
The front door leads directly into a large parlor, size 15 feet by 13 feet 6 inches. Directly to the rear is located a large dining room with cased opening. Dining room is 18 feet long by 13 feet wide, has a sideboard and is trimmed with plate rail. To the rear of this room is the kitchen, size 10 feet by 10 feet, with a door leading to the rear porch. The pantry being located between the kitchen and dining room makes it possible to use this room as a butler's serving pantry. On the left side of the house are located two large and airy chambers, size 13 feet by 13 feet 6 inches, with closets, and conveniently located. Between the two chambers is a bathroom, size 9 feet 6 inches by 9 feet 6 inches.

For the front door we furnish a heavy bevel plate glass. Interior doors are five-cross panel yellow pine with clear yellow pine casings and trim throughout. Interior can be finished either light or dark finish. Clear yellow pine for the floors for the entire house and porches.
Built on concrete foundation. No. 1 yellow pine framing lumber. Sided with wide cypress siding (or shingles if preferred), and has a cedar shingle roof. Basement excavated and has concrete floor.

Height of Ceiling.
Basement, 7 feet from floor to joists.
First floor, 9 feet from floor to ceiling.

This house can be built on a lot 40 feet wide.

If estimates and specifications for plumbing, hot water, steam or hot air heating systems are desired write for them, mentioning Modern Home No. C172 or No. C2025 in your request.

SEARS, ROEBUCK AND CO., CHICAGO, ILLINOIS

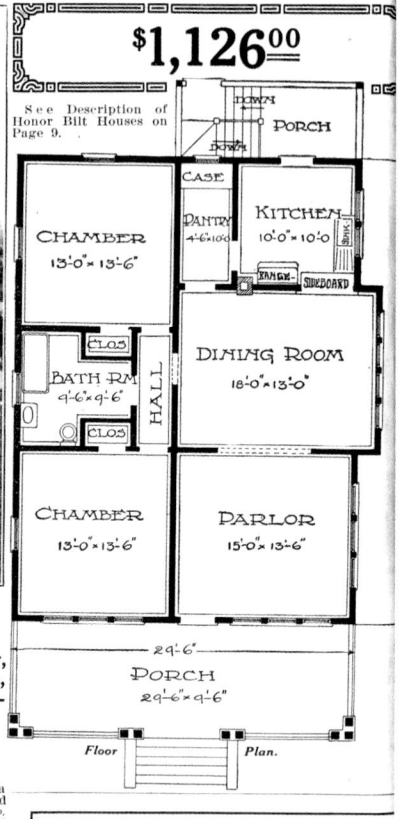

Prettiest of 200 Bungalows.

Bay Shore, N. Y.
Sears, Roebuck and Co., Chicago, Ill.
Gentlemen:—Under separate cover I am sending you a photo of my house, No. C172. I am well pleased with my bungalow and it is considered the prettiest one in this vicinity and there are about 200 nearby. I probably saved $200.00 and got better material.
Very truly yours,
C. L. DeWITTA.

—48—

Top: The Hazleton was a popular house for Sears, and here's one in Tamms (in southern Illinois). Note the curious little side window in the dining room bay. I think of the Hazleton as my "house of threes"—three windows flanking the door, three windows in the shed dormer and six windows in the dining room bay.

Bottom: A near-perfect Hazleton in Edwardsville. The four windows in the attic have been added.

Bungalow (One-and-a-Half-Story)

BUNGALOW (ONE-AND-A-HALF-STORY)

Notice the long, sloping lines of the front porch gable on this Kilbourne. The original floor plan calls for the space occupied by the small dormer to be a closet. (Elmhurst)

134

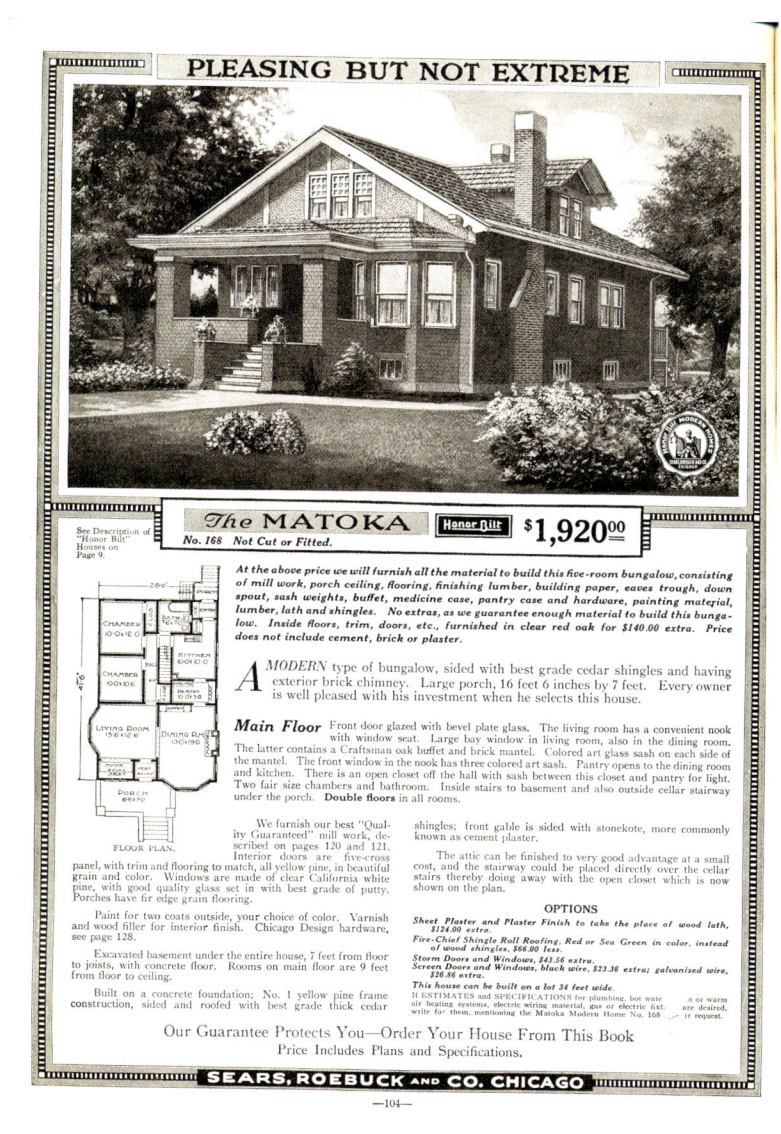

Surprisingly spacious, the Matoka had bay windows on the front and side, with space for a couple bedrooms on the second floor. (St. Charles)

Bungalow (One-and-a-Half-Story)

BUNGALOW (ONE-AND-A-HALF-STORY)

FIVE ROOMS BATH AND PORCH

The Marina
No. 7024 "Already Cut" and Fitted, $1,888.00 As shown above.
No. 2024 "Already Cut" and Fitted, with Exterior as shown below, $1,661.00

At the prices quoted we will furnish all the material to build this five-room house with bath, consisting of mill work, medicine case, flooring, porch ceiling, siding, finishing lumber, kitchen cupboard, building paper, eaves trough, down spout, sash weights, hardware, nails, painting material, roofing, lumber and lath. We guarantee enough material to build this house. Prices do not include cement, brick or plaster.

This house can be built with the rooms reversed. See page 3.

THIS house is quite out of the ordinary in many respects. Note the concrete block posts surmounted by graceful wood columns. The paneled stucco porch gable adds much to the appearance and the Fire-Chief Shingle Roll Roofing sets off the house to the best advantage.

First Floor A large living room occupies about one-half of the first floor, extending across the entire width of the house. Cased opening between the living room and dining room. Beamed ceiling in the dining room. Door leads from dining room into the kitchen. A stairway leads from the dining room to the second floor. Stairs lead from kitchen to basement. A large cupboard in kitchen serves as a pantry. Rooms are 8 feet 4 inches from floor to ceiling.

Second Floor Two good size bedrooms with closet. Each closet has a sash for light and ventilation. Both bedrooms and bathroom are well lighted and ventilated. Rooms are 8 feet from floor to ceiling.

Basement Excavated basement under rear half of house with concrete floor, lighted with basement sash. Height of basement, 7 feet from floor to joists.

We furnish our best "Quality Guaranteed" mill work, shown on pages 108 and 109. Interior doors are five-cross panel, with trim and flooring to match. All yellow pine, in beautiful grain and color. Windows are made of clear California white pine, with good quality glass set in with best grade of putty. Porches have fir edge grain flooring.

Paint for three coats outside, your choice of color. Varnish and wood filler for interior finish. Stratford Design hardware, see page 117.

"Honor Bilt" No. 1 yellow pine frame construction, sided with narrow bevel clear cypress siding, 90-Pound Fire-Chief Shingle Roll Roofing for roof and porches, guaranteed for seventeen years. Concrete block foundation.

OPTIONS
Sheet Plaster and Plaster Finish to take the place of wood lath, $86.00 extra. See page 114.
Oak Doors, Oak Trim, Oak Floors for living room and dining room, $140.00 extra.
Maple Flooring furnished for kitchen and bathroom instead of yellow pine, no extra charge.
Storm Doors and Windows, $75.00 extra.
Screen Doors and Windows, black wire, $38.00 extra; galvanized wire, $41.00 extra.
Double Doors furnished for "Honor Bilt" Homes.

For Price of Plumbing, Heating, Wiring, Electric Fixtures and Shades, see page 115.

Our Guarantee Protects You—Order Your House From This Book.
Prices Include Plans and Specifications.

This house furnished with exterior as shown in this picture for $1,661.00. If wanted this way order No. 2024.

Page 52.

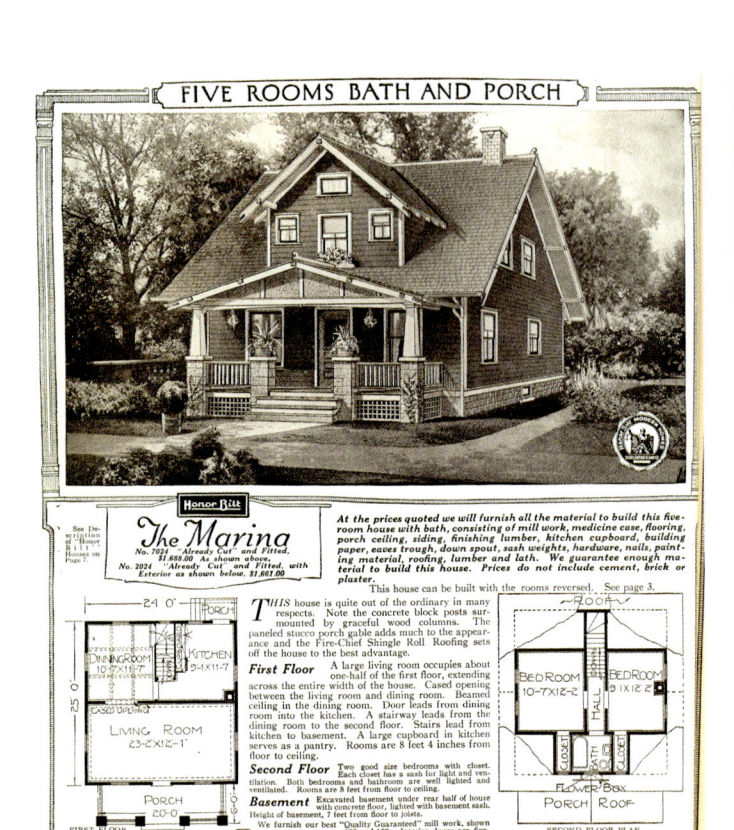

SEARS, ROEBUCK AND CO., CHICAGO-PHILADELPHIA

INTERIORS – The MARINA

The Living Room
Needs Only the Musician to Make It "Home, Sweet Home."

The Dining Room
If You Like Beamed Ceilings This Room Will Appeal to You.

The Kitchen

IN CONSIDERING our prices, it will pay you to note carefully the bills of material. For instance, note the big cupboard in the kitchen above. This is furnished by us and makes a pantry unnecessary, thereby saving many steps.

Don't forget that quality of material is of far greater importance than price. Most people build only once in a lifetime and if quality is neglected to make a temporary saving, the upkeep in a very few years will more than offset the saving in the original cost. From the foundation to the roof, from the framing lumber to the last coat of paint, we guarantee everything that goes into the construction of our "Honor Bilt" Modern Homes to be the best of its kind. We want every purchaser of an "Honor Bilt" Modern Home to be a perfectly satisfied customer and we aim to give him a house that will last for a lifetime.

SEARS, ROEBUCK AND CO. CHICAGO

—45—

136

Pretty in pink, this Marina is in excellent condition and looks much like it did when built in the late 1910s. (Alton)

Bungalow (One-and-a-Half-Story)

BUNGALOW (ONE-AND-A-HALF-STORY)

A distinctive feature of the Solace is those three windows on the right side, descending in size. The first window was the bedroom, next was the bath and the last window was for the kitchen. The original pergola on the front porch of the Solace rarely endures through the years. (Wheaton)

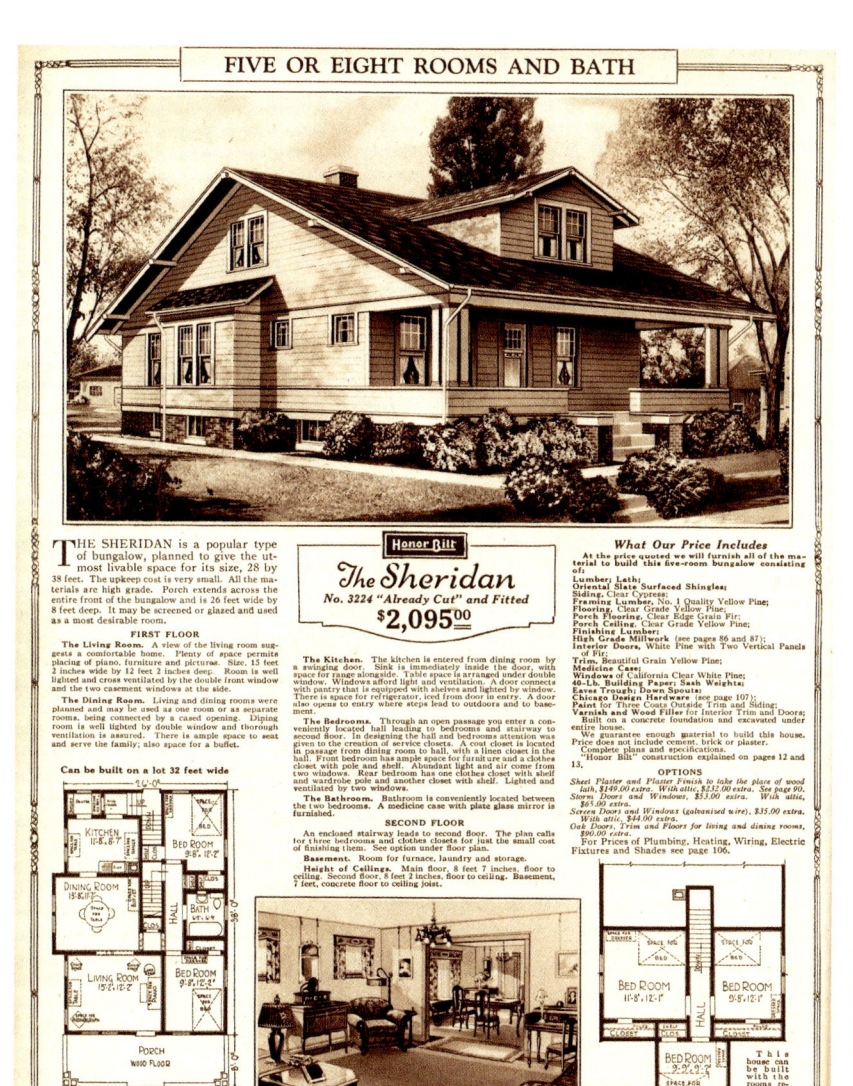

Not surprisingly, Cairo has an abundance of Sears homes. Here's a Sheridan that (unfortunately) has been turned into a duplex.

Bungalow (One-and-a-Half-Story)

BUNGALOW (ONE-AND-A-HALF-STORY)

An entire second floor was added to this Avondale in Elmhurst. Note that the roofline and the eaves mirror that of the original house. This is a fine example of a thoughtful remodeling, as it retains the old home's original flair and style.

With its long, low hip roof and exaggerated eaves, this Avondale might be described as a bungalow with many prairie-type features. The Avondale was one of Sears's most popular homes. In the 1950s or '60s, a slick salesman probably talked the homeowner into covering up that old wooden siding with some low-maintenance "never need painting" shingles. (Litchfield)

Bungalow (One-and-a-Half-Story)

Bungalow (One-and-a-Half-Story)

The catalog picture of the traditional Sears Hollywood.

Close-up of the "alternate" Sears Hollywood (from right-hand corner of the 1919 catalog page).

This Hollywood appears to be suffering from a flesh-eating disease and has lost most of its skin. Despite years of neglect, it's still clinging to life. Try this with a McMansion and you'll have nothing left but drywall dust and galvanized nails. (Owaneco)

142

Using grantee records, Rebecca Hunter authenticated this as a Sears Hollywood. It may have been customized when built, or dramatically altered in later years, but it lacks many of the visual clues of the Hollywood.

BUNGALOW (ONE-AND-A-HALF-STORY)

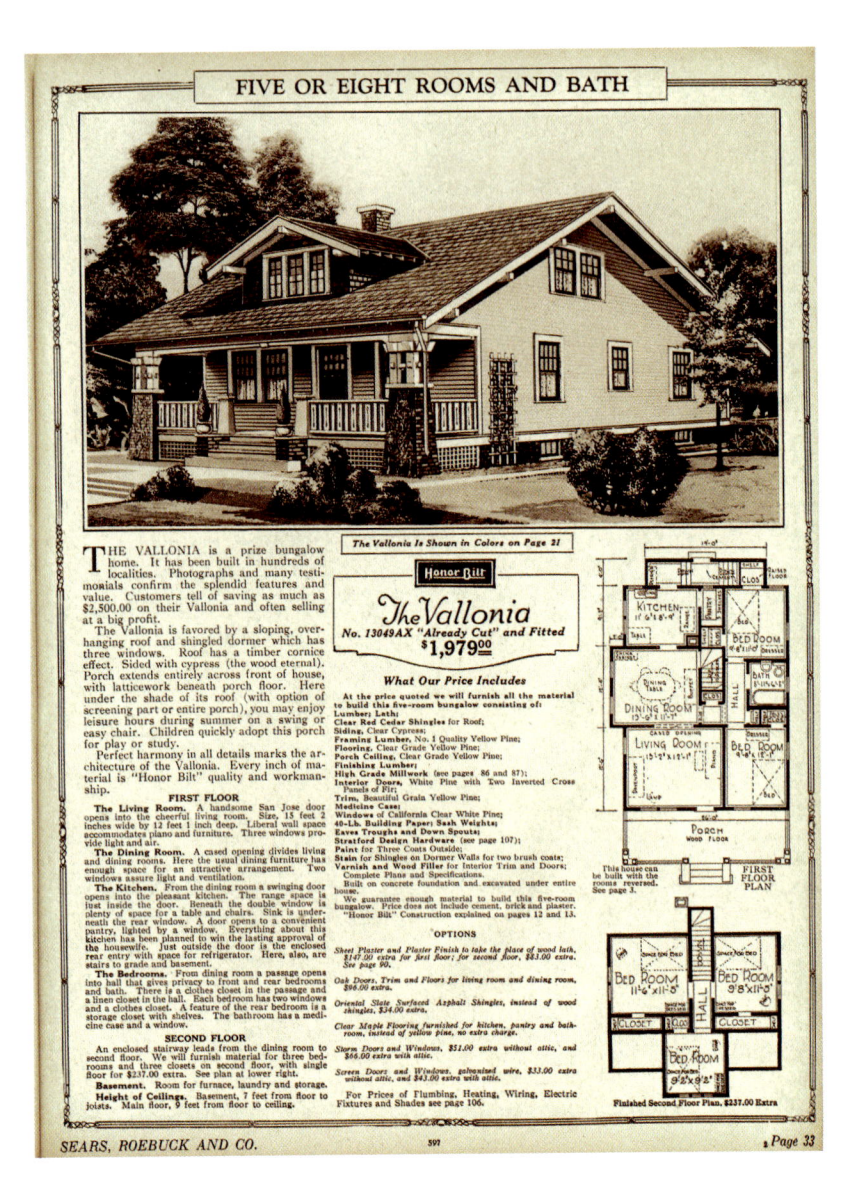

A fine-looking Vallonia in Grafton with its original casement windows in the gabled dormer. Notice the intricate columns on the front porch. The design of these columns was not unique to Sears, but it's one of those signs that suggests a closer look is in order. Two dozen of Sears's most popular designs featured these columns.

144

Best known as the home of Superman, Metropolis, Illinois, is also the home to several Sears homes, including this Sears Westly. Unlike many Westlys, this one still has its original railing on both the second-floor and first-floor porch.

BUNGALOW (ONE-AND-A-HALF-STORY)

BUNGALOW (ONE-AND-A-HALF-STORY)

The front porch has been enclosed, but other than that, this Princeville still looks much like the original catalog page. (West Chicago)

This Princeville in St. Charles bears little resemblance to its original form. Somewhere in this modern dwelling is a dandy Sears Princeville begging to be released. Rebecca Hunter found this house through grantee records.

Bungalow
(Two-Story)

Bungalows come in all shapes and sizes, and there are a few that are two stories tall, such as the kit homes included in this grouping. The defining features that characterize these two-story homes as bungalows are the exposed rafter tails, oversized eaves supported by triangular brackets, simple rooflines and full-width porches.

In spite of the vinyl siding and replacement windows, this Edgemere still looks just like the catalog image from the 1916 catalog. (Livingston)

BUNGALOW (TWO-STORY)

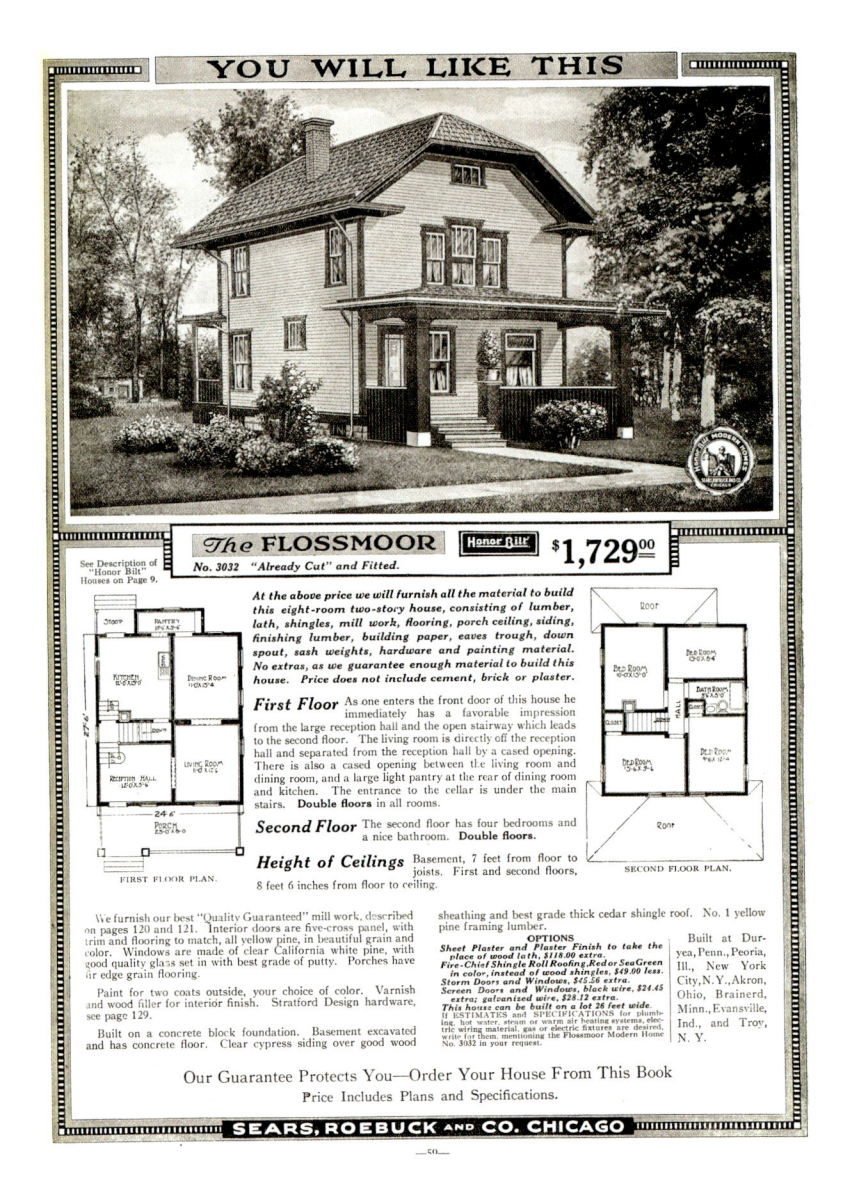

The three contiguous windows on the home's front and the clipped gable roofline give this Flossmoor its distinctive look. (Batavia)

150

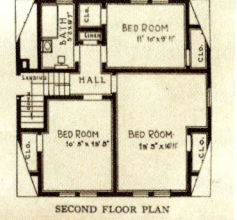

The Homewood was apparently not a big seller for Sears. This one in Elmhurst is the only example of this model I've ever seen.

Bungalow (Two-Story)

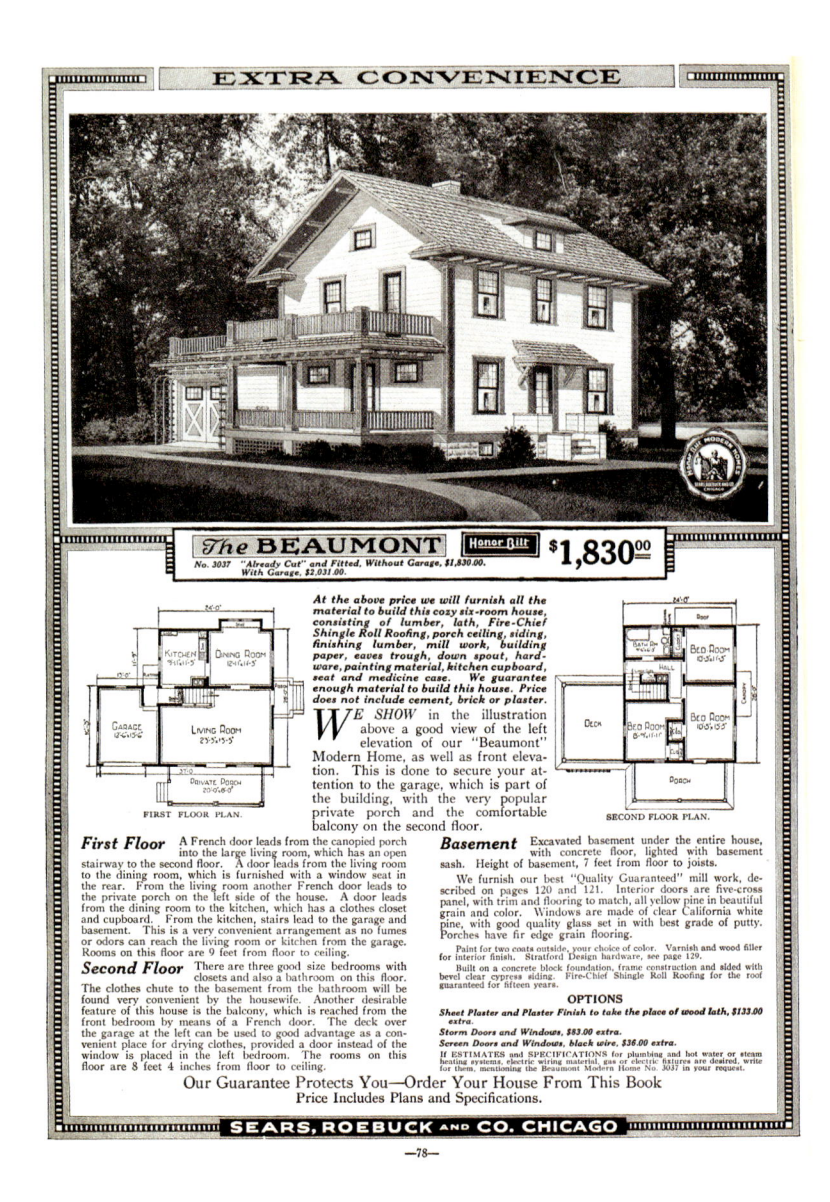

Dentil molding and bracketed eaves complement this Beaumont in Carlinville. This home sits a few blocks away from "Standard Addition," a working-class neighborhood with more than 150 Sears homes.

Casey is an old railroad town with many examples of Sears Modern Homes, including this Sears Arlington. A few of the original windows (nine over one) remain.

BUNGALOW (TWO-STORY)

BUNGALOW (TWO-STORY)

One of the twenty-three Sears homes on Ninth Street (in Wood River), this Roanoke is covered with a whole lot of vinyl and plastic. The PVC fish scales in the front gable would be more appropriate in a nineteenth-century home (if they were wood, that is).

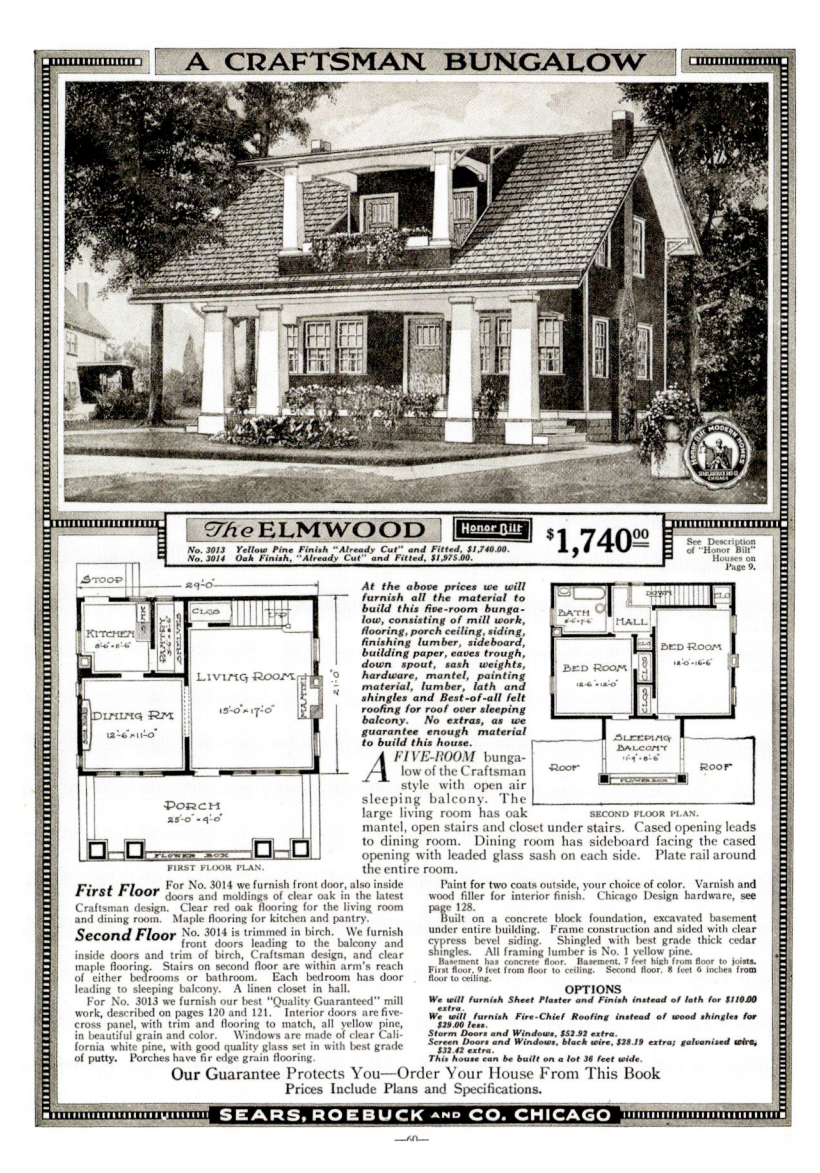

Originally, the shed dormer on the Sunbeam's front served as a sleeping porch, accessible from both upstairs bedrooms. Today, it's very unusual to find a Sears Sunbeam (also called an Elmwood) with the sleeping porch still open and original. (Nashville)

Bungalow (Two-Story)

Foursquare

For both city lots and spacious farms, the American Foursquare was extremely popular from the late 1800s to the 1930s. Sears offered many Foursquares, probably because these houses were quite spacious, very simple and easy for the novice homebuilder. The cube-shape house featured squared-off interior spaces, too. The four corners of the first floor contained an entry foyer, living room, dining room and kitchen. Upstairs, four corners housed a bath and three bedrooms. Most Sears Foursquares had an oversized hipped dormer in the attic with a wee tiny window at its center, which is a distinctive feature that can help identify a Sears home.

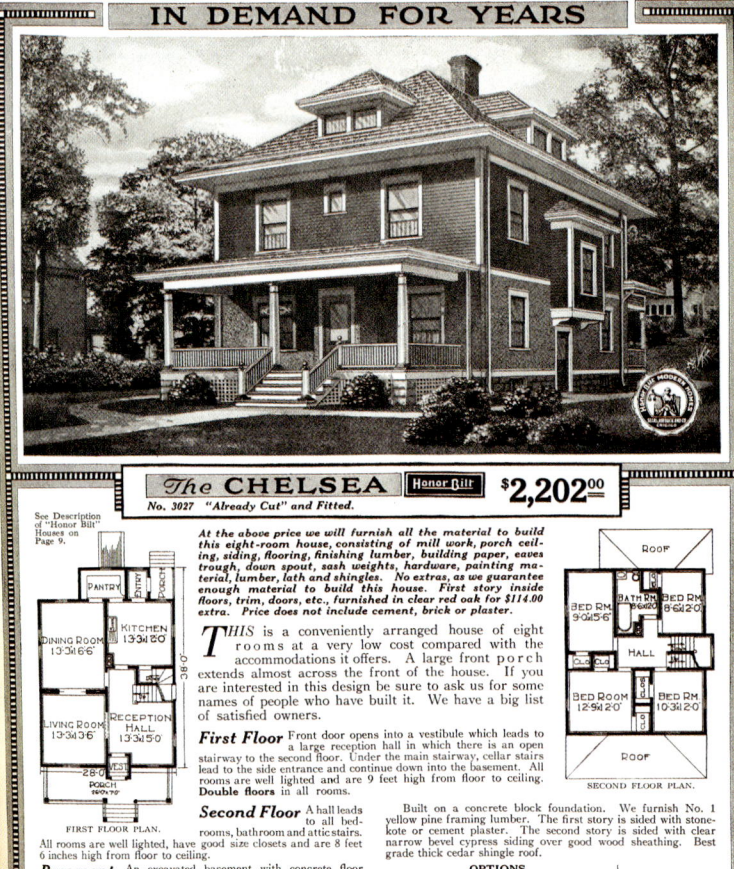

One of several Foursquares that Sears offered, the front porch on this Chelsea has been enclosed, and the eaves were wrapped in aluminum, but that original closet window (center, second floor) is still in place. These are often closed in to create more closet space.

FOURSQUARE

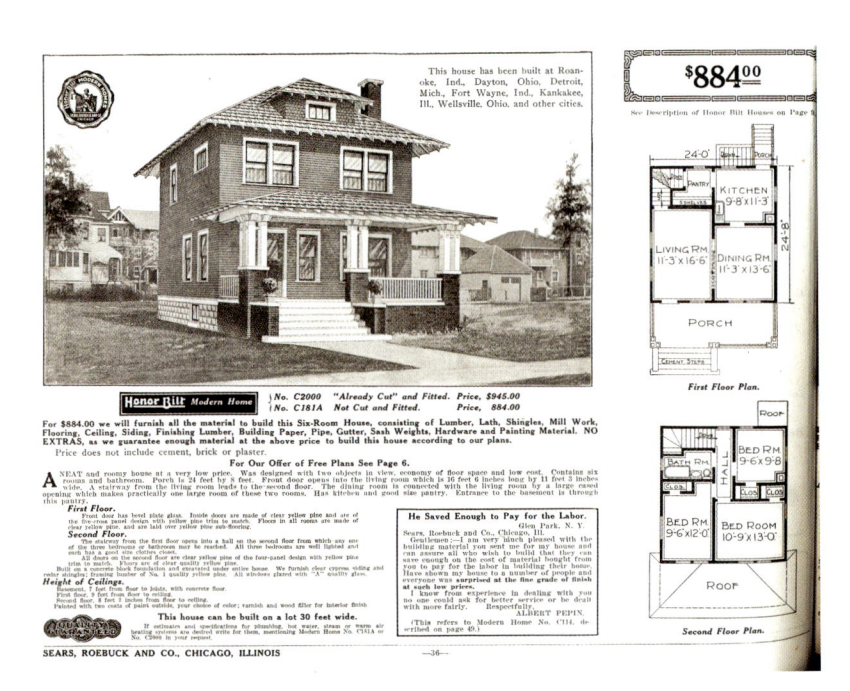

A happy Gladstone sits in Champaign, Illinois, looking much like it did when built eight decades ago. The unique front porch columns and oversized dormer with its wee tiny window is a key feature in identifying the Gladstone.

158

Accessible from two upstairs bedrooms, this covered balcony remains open and intact on Modern Home #163. Note the stair-step windows on the side, the exaggerated gabled dormer and oversized hip roof. (Taylorville)

FOURSQUARE

FOURSQUARE

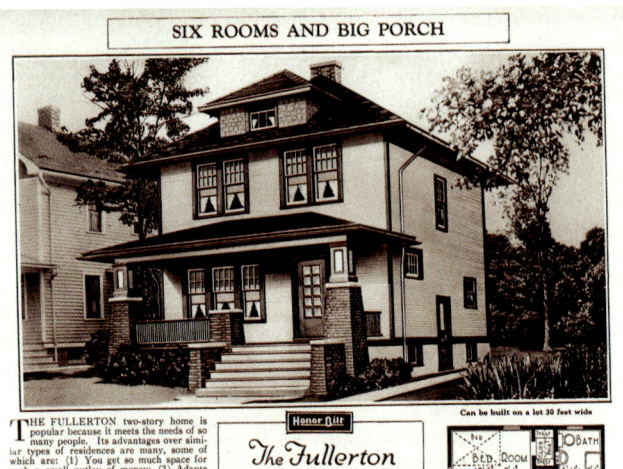

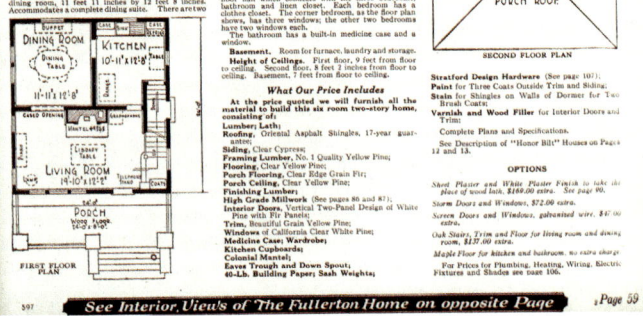

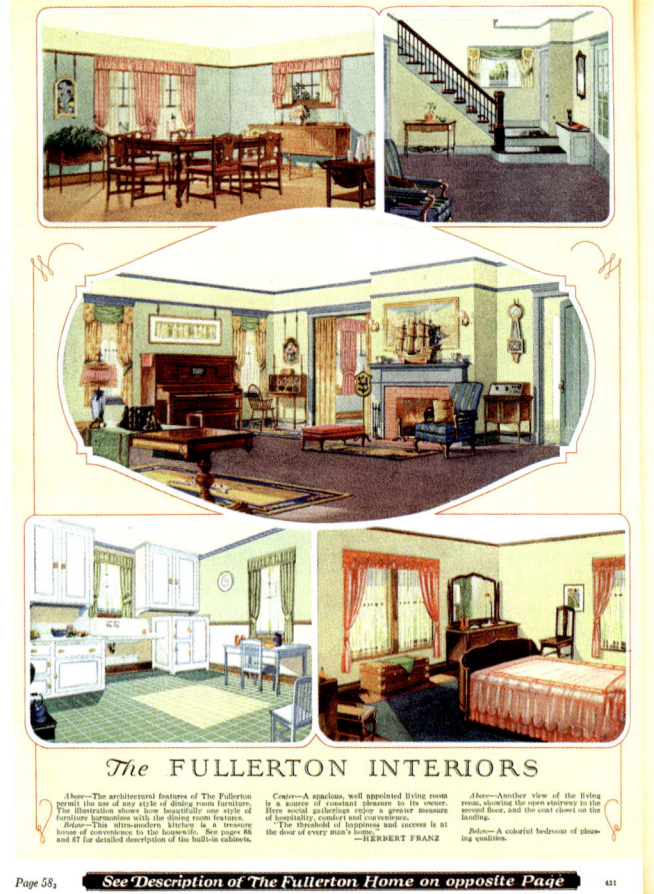

One of the original twenty-three houses in a row on Wood River's Ninth Street, this was the only Fullerton in Standard Oil's $1 million order.

FOURSQUARE

FOURSQUARE

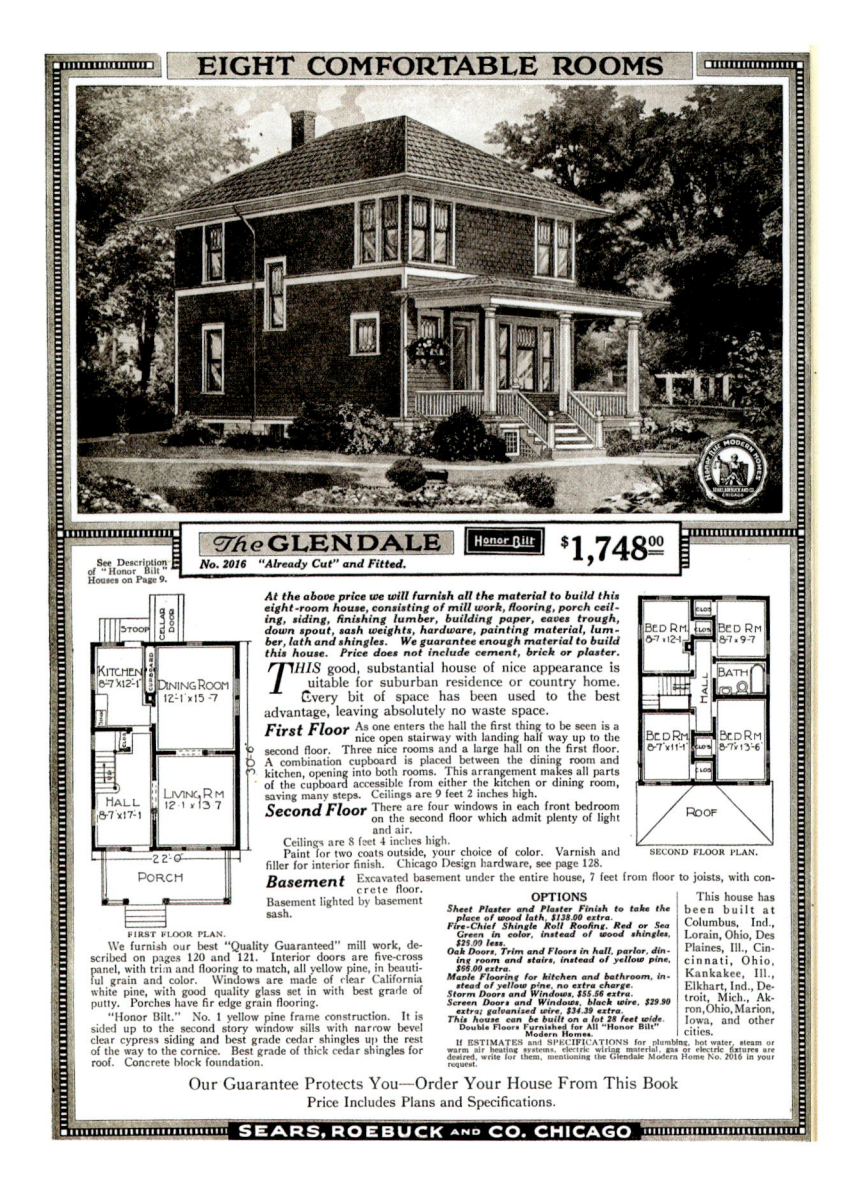

Located in Mounds (near Cairo), this forlorn Glendale still retains many of its original features. However, if you decide to check it out, stay away from the backyard. There's a very angry sixty-pound pitbull chained to the back porch pier, just waiting to lunge at curious house hunters. Ask me how I know this.

The two-story bay window and the deep, inset attic window are key features for identifying this Whitehall (top, left). Another very popular model for Sears.

The Whitehall at bottom left is in Wood River and is feeling some pain. Faux logs plus oversized replacement windows on historically significant homes equals depressingly unattractive.

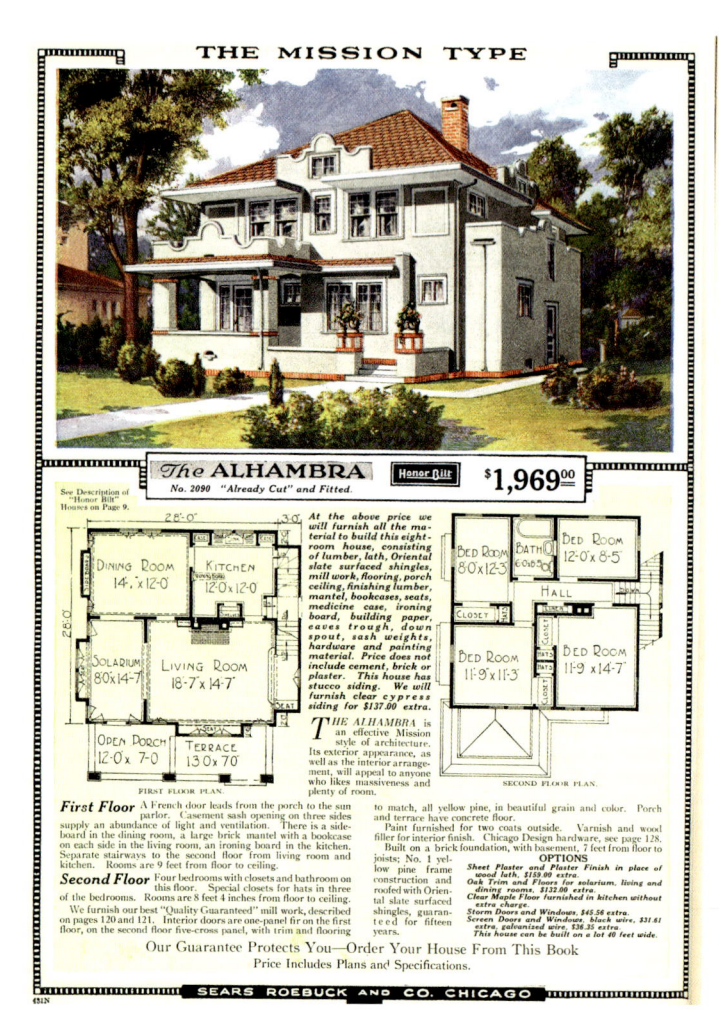

FOURSQUARE

THE MISSION TYPE

The ALHAMBRA
No. 2090 "Already Cut" and Fitted. Honor Bilt $1,969.00

At the above price we will furnish all the material to build this eight-room house, consisting of lumber, lath, Oriental slate surfaced shingles, mill work, flooring, porch ceiling, finishing lumber, mantel, bookcases, seats, medicine case, ironing board, building paper, eaves trough, down spout, sash weights, hardware and painting material. Price does not include cement, brick or plaster. This house has stucco siding. We will furnish clear cypress siding for $137.00 extra.

THE ALHAMBRA is an effective Mission style of architecture. Its exterior appearance, as well as the interior arrangement, will appeal to anyone who likes massiveness and plenty of room.

First Floor A French door leads from the porch to the sun parlor. Casement sash opening on three sides supply an abundance of light and ventilation. There is a sideboard in the dining room, a large brick mantel with a bookcase on each side in the living room, an ironing board in the kitchen. Separate stairways to the second floor from living room and kitchen. Rooms are 9 feet from floor to ceiling.

Second Floor Four bedrooms with closets and bathroom on this floor. Special closets for hats in three of the bedrooms. Rooms are 8 feet 4 inches from floor to ceiling. We furnish our best "Quality Guaranteed" mill work, described on pages 120 and 121. Interior doors are one-panel fir on the first floor, on the second floor five-cross panel, with trim and flooring to match, all yellow pine, in beautiful grain and color. Porch and terrace have concrete floor.

Paint furnished for two coats outside. Varnish and wood filler for interior finish. Chicago Design hardware, see page 128.

Built on a brick foundation, with basement, 7 feet from floor to joists; No. 1 yellow pine frame construction and roofed with Oriental slate surfaced shingles, guaranteed for fifteen years.

OPTIONS
Sheet Plaster and Plaster Finish in place of wood lath, $159.00 extra.
Oak Trim and Floors for solarium, living and dining rooms, $132.00 extra.
Clear Maple Floor furnished in kitchen without extra charge.
Storm Doors and Windows, $45.56 extra.
Screen Doors and Windows, black wire, $31.61 extra, galvanized wire, $36.35 extra.
This house can be built on a lot 40 feet wide.

Our Guarantee Protects You—Order Your House From This Book
Price Includes Plans and Specifications.

SEARS ROEBUCK AND CO. CHICAGO

INTERIORS – The ALHAMBRA

The Living Room
A suggestion for interior treatment that will be helpful to the housewife.

The Dining Room
What a wealth of warm hospitality this picture reveals.

The Sun Parlor
In this illustration the beautiful foliage outside seems to vie with the rich furnishings in harmony of color and richness of contrast.

A recognized authority on interior decoration writes: "Brilliant colors are used in a room exactly as a painter puts the finishing touches of high lights in a picture. They have a magical touch, but, like all magical things, must be used with the utmost care and restraint. Fortunately, a greater appreciation of the value of strong color is evident every year. In planning the color treatment of a room it should be considered as a whole, remembering that every color introduced will have its effect upon the other colors. Far more effect may be obtained by color than by ornament. As the effect is greater, so greater care should be taken in using color in decoration. The first consideration in choosing the color scheme for a room is the exposure of the room. If it faces North or East, warm tints should be used—something that will give full value to all the light that gets to the room. Conversely, a color that absorbs light should be avoided—red or dark blue, for example. The craze for neutral colored backgrounds has led us into the fallacy of using a putty color or blend in all rooms, regardless of their exposure. This is a pity, since a North room so needs the artificial glow from a warm tinted background. The suitable colors for a North or East room are tan, buff, brown, rose, apricot or pink, or these combined with one another or with a cool tone. The room with the Southern or Western exposure requires a more neutral toned background—gray, putty color, white and black, blue-green, mauve or mulberry; in fact, any shade that has of itself a cool effect. In these rooms the purpose is to counteract the excess of sunlight and glare and their subsequent effect on the nerves. For color reacts on us in an extraordinary way. Too much brilliant color excites and tires us and too drab colors give us no stimulus."

SEARS ROEBUCK AND CO. CHICAGO

164

This Alhambra in Peotone is in very good condition and retains the original parapet around the front porch roof and dormers, accented by a dark brown trim. *Courtesy of Dale Patrick Wolicki.*

Other Styles

The homes included in this grouping have stylistic features that reflect several architectural elements and can't be easily characterized.

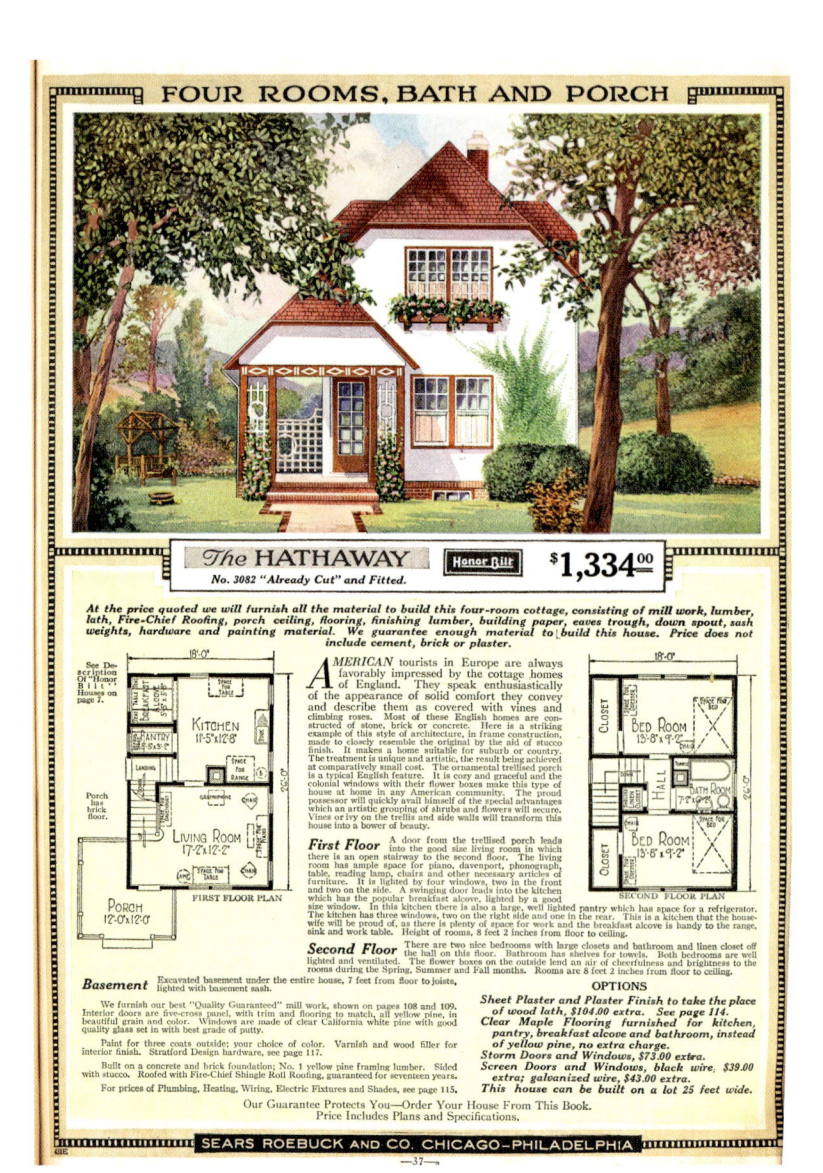

Years ago, a woman called to tell me that she lived in the "Halfway House," built by Sears. A few days later, she sent me a photo of the house, and I saw that it was indeed a Sears house, the "Hathaway." Despite the many modifications to this little brick home in Elmhurst, it's still easily identifiable as a Sears Hathaway.

Other Styles

No. 6013A FOUR ROOMS AND BATH, $474.00

THE HUDSON
Standard Built

No. 6013A—"Hudson" 4 Rooms and Bath

$474.00

At the price quoted we will furnish all the material to build this four-room house with bath, No. 6013A, consisting of lumber, lath, millwork, flooring, porch ceiling, siding, finishing lumber, millwork, slate surfaced roofing, hardware and paint. We guarantee enough material to build this house. Price does not include cement, brick or plaster.

No. 6013—Already Cut and Fitted

$636.00

At the price quoted we will furnish all material to build this four-room house with bath, No. 6013, consisting of lumber, lath, millwork, flooring, porch ceiling, shingles, siding, finishing lumber, tarred felt, hardware and painting material. We guarantee enough material to build this house. Price does not include cement, brick or plaster.

OPTIONS

Storm Doors and Windows, $30.00 extra for No. 6013; $25.00 extra for No. 6013A.
Screen Doors and Windows, galvanized wire, $23.00 extra for No. 6013; $20.00 extra for No. 6013A.
Front and rear steps for No. 6013A, $8.00 extra.
Wood shingles instead of slate surfaced roofing for No. 6013A, $20.00 extra.
Tarred felt under floor and siding for No. 6013A, $12.00 extra.

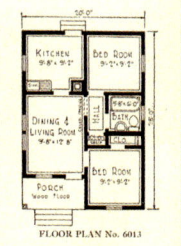

THE HUDSON Standard Built Home is an investment that readily appeals to the thrifty family. Here is everything one expects in a modest and up to date house. Consider the good quality material and construction and low price! The Hudson was planned by us after many comparisons of designs. All the material comes from our own large mills and yards. No middleman's profits.

The exterior presents a neat and becoming appearance. The porch is sheltered underneath the main roof of the house.

The Living Room. From the porch a door opens into the living room. Size, 9 feet 5 inches by 10 feet 7 inches. There's ample wall space for a piano and furniture. A side window provides light and ventilation.

The Kitchen. From the living room a door opens into the kitchen. Size, 9 feet 5 inches by 9 feet 5 inches. It has plenty of space for sink, stove, kitchen table and ice box. Light and air from one window. A door leads to the rear yard.

The Bedrooms. The front bedroom is entered from the living room. A front window supplies light and air.

The rear bedroom is entered from the kitchen. One window supplies light and air.

The Bathroom is entered from the living room. Plumbing fixtures may be roughed-in on one wall, saving on installation.

This Standard-Built Hudson (Sears economy line) is so plain and simple that I would have never discovered it through a windshield survey. This house was found after I did a check of the grantee records in Madison County. The small front porch has been enclosed, and an addition has been added to the rear. When built, the house had a mere 560 square feet and two bedrooms, both measuring 9 feet, 2 inches square. (Alton)

The double-entrance porch and long, tall vent on the front wall are key features of the Berwyn. Other than the addition of shingled siding, this house probably looks much like it did when built in the late '20s or early '30s. (Elgin)

OTHER STYLES

FOR TOWN OR COUNTRY

The KISMET — Honor Bilt — $806.00
No. 2002 "Already Cut" and Fitted.

See Description of "Honor Bilt" Houses on Page 9.

At the above price we will furnish all the material to build this four-room bungalow, consisting of lumber, lath, shingles, mill work, porch ceiling, siding, flooring, finishing lumber, building paper, eaves trough, down spout, sash weights, hardware and painting material. We guarantee enough material to build this house. Price does not include cement, brick or plaster.

IN THIS bungalow we offer a home at a low price with an absolute guarantee as to the quality of the materials we furnish. This four-room bungalow is suitable for almost any location. In many sections a four or five-room cottage and lot will sell for $2,000.00 to $2,500.00. Notwithstanding the low price which we ask for all of the material required in the construction of this bungalow, there is no sacrifice of quality and there will be no shortage of material. We furnish a double floor, also good wood sheathing, and plenty of building paper so that the house will be perfectly comfortable in the coldest weather. As this house can be built on a lot 25 feet wide, it is suitable for town or country. For a farm house, for a small family, it represents a splendid investment. It is gracefully proportioned and when nicely painted will look well in any community.

Main Floor A glazed front door opens into the living room. A door leads from the living room to front bedroom, and doors lead from the dining room to the kitchen, doors lead into the rear bedroom and bathroom. Two good size closets. Rooms are 9 feet from floor to ceiling.

We furnish our best "Quality Guaranteed" mill work, described on pages 120 and 121. Interior doors are five-cross panel, with trim and flooring to match, all yellow pine, in beautiful grain and color. Windows are made of clear California white pine, with good quality glass set in with best grade of putty. Porches have fir edge grain flooring.

Paint for two coats outside, your choice of color. Varnish and wood filler for interior finish. Stratford Design hardware, see page 129.

Built on a concrete block foundation, excavated basement. "Honor Bilt" frame construction and sided with narrow bevel clear cypress siding. Best grade thick cedar shingle roof. All framing timbers are of No. 1 quality yellow pine.

This house has been built at Culver, Ind., Hamilton, Ind., Aurora, Ill., Cleveland, Ohio, Havana, Ill., Elkhart, Ind., Greenfield, Ohio, and other cities.

OPTIONS
Sheet Plaster and Plaster Finish to take the place of wood lath, $54.00 extra.
Fire-Chief Shingle Roll Roofing, Red or Sea Green in color, instead of wood shingles, $23.00 less.
Storm Doors and Windows, $23.56 extra.
Screen Doors and Windows, black wire, $12.46 extra; galvanized wire, $14.33 extra.
This house can be built on a lot 25 feet wide.
If ESTIMATES and SPECIFICATIONS for plumbing, hot water, steam or warm air heating systems, electric wiring material, gas or electric fixtures are desired, write for them, mentioning the Kismet Modern Home No. 2002 in your request.

Our Guarantee Protects You—Order Your House From This Book
Price Includes Plans and Specifications.

SEARS, ROEBUCK AND CO. CHICAGO

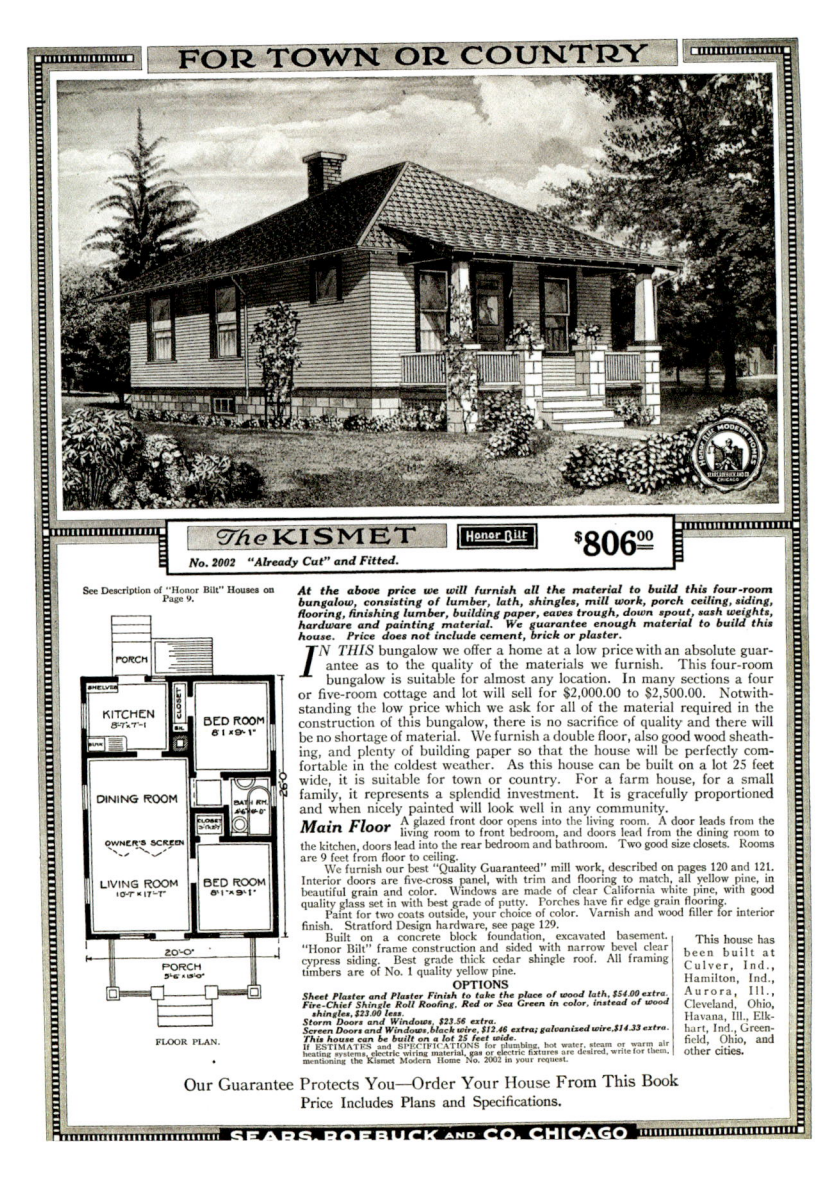

This little Sears Kismet originally had an exterior footprint of 20 by 26 feet, a mere 520 square feet of living space. The 75-square-foot porch has been enclosed, and a small addition has been added to the rear. (Elmhurst)

170

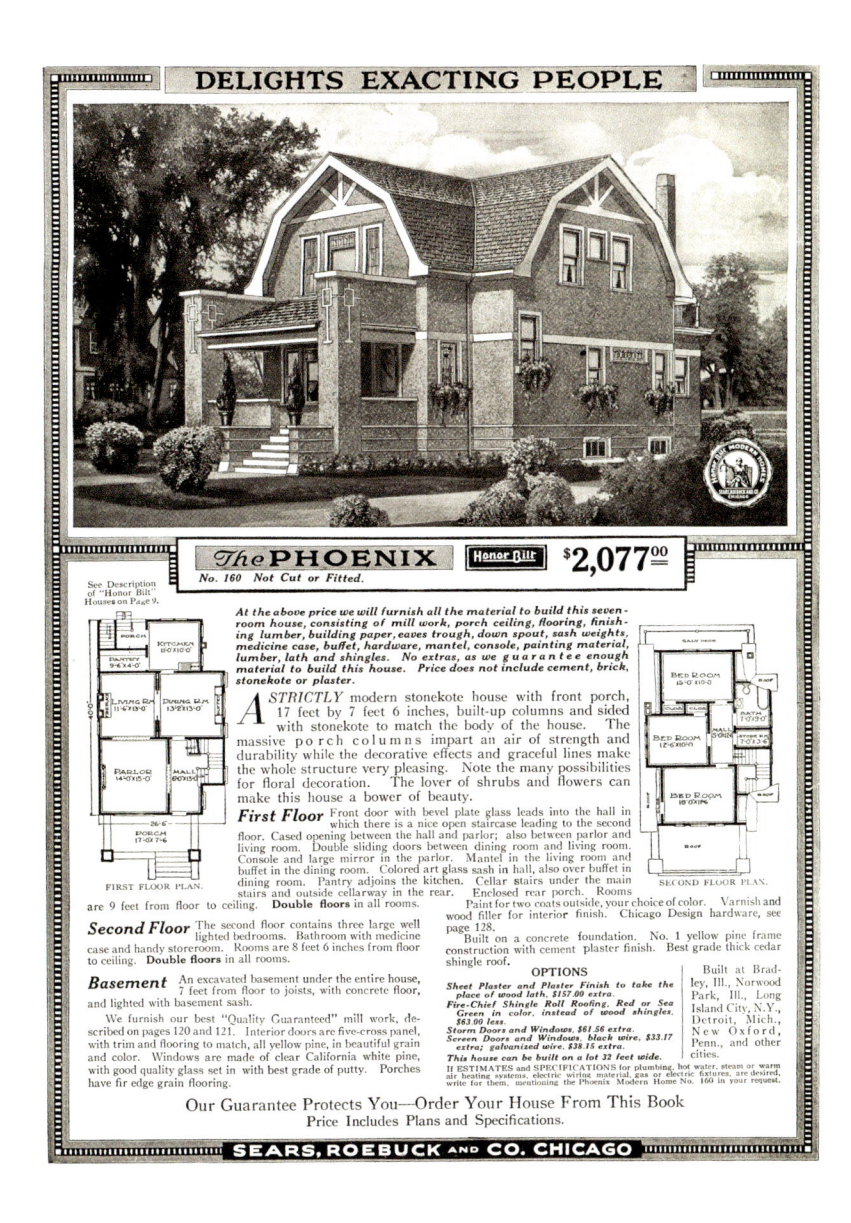

Does this Phoenix delight exacting people? So promises the catalog page. Look closely and you'll see the architectural details atop the squared front columns. In my travels, I've only seen three Phoenixes, and this one is in Newman. *Courtesy of Rebecca Hunter.*

OTHER STYLES

171

OTHER STYLES

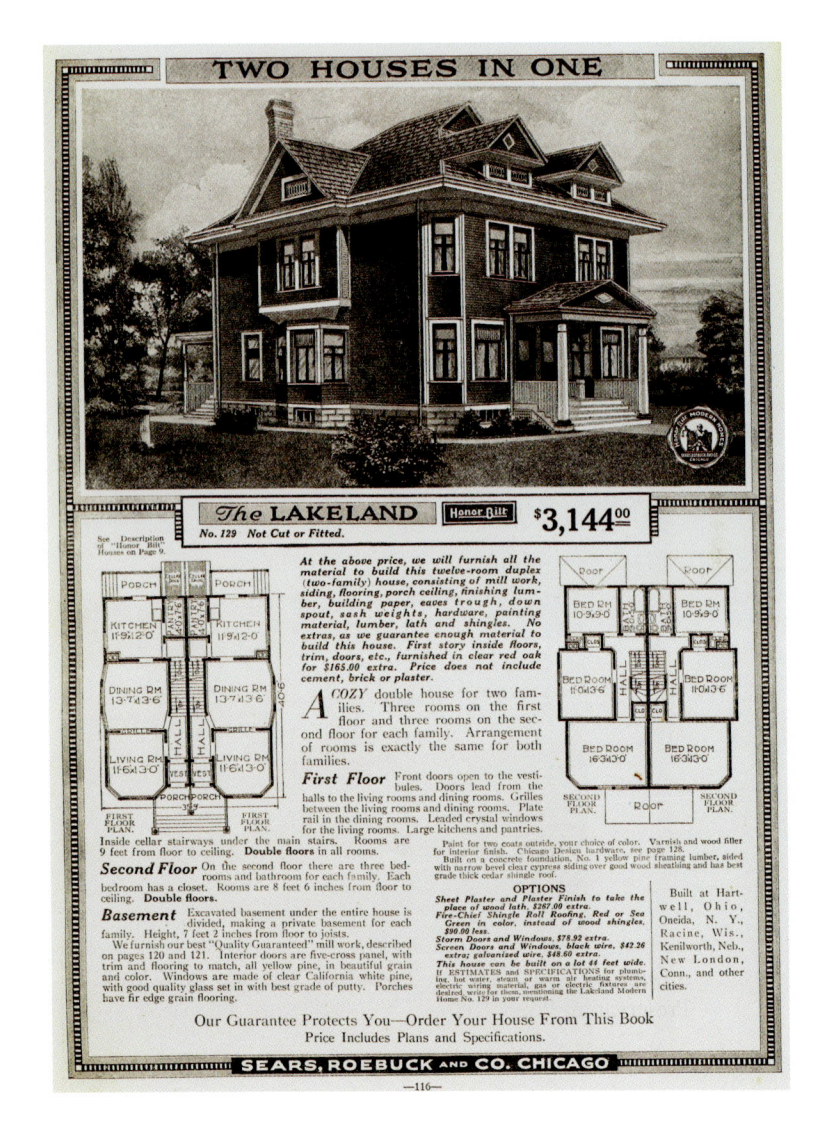

Sears did duplexes, too. Other than the satellite dish by the front porch, this Sears Lakeland in Alton looks much like it did when built in the late 1910s or early '20s.

172

Bibliography

Books

Bruce, Alfred and Harold Sandbank. *A History of Prefabrication*. Raritan, NJ: John B. Pierce Foundation Housing Research Division, 1945.

Carlinville and Macoupin County Sesquicentennial, Inc. *The Story of Macoupin County, 1829–1979*. Carlinville, IL: Carlinville and Macoupin County Sesquicentennial, Inc., 1979.

Clark, Clifford Edward, Jr. *The American Family Home, 1800–1960*. Chapel Hill: University of North Carolina Press, 1986.

Dover Publishing. *Small Houses of the Twenties, The Sears Roebuck 1926 House Catalog, An Unabridged Reprint*. New York: Dover Publications, Inc., 1991.

Emmet, Boris, and John E. Jeuck. *Catalogues and Counters, A History of Sears, Roebuck and Company*. Chicago: University of Chicago Press, 1950.

Gowans, Alan. *The Comfortable House, North American Suburban Architecture, 1890–1930*. Cambridge, MA: MIT Press, 1986.

Hoge, Cecil C., Jr. *The First Hundred Years Are the Toughest: What We Can Learn from the Century of Competition Between Sears and Wards*. Berkeley, CA: Ten Speed Press, 1988.

Hunter, Rebecca. *Elgin Illinois Sears House Research Project*. Elgin, IL: 2003. (Available for interlibrary loan from the Gail Borden Public Library in Elgin, Illinois.)

Katz, Donald R. *The Big Store, Inside the Crisis and Revolution at Sears*. New York: Viking Penguin Inc., 1987.

Nye, David E. *Electrifying America, Social Meanings of a New Technology*. Cambridge, MA: MIT Press, 1990.

Schiffer Publishing Ltd. *Homes in a Box, Modern Homes from Sears Roebuck*. Atglen, PA: Schiffer Publishing Ltd., 1998.

Smith, LaWanda. *The History of Wood River, Illinois*. Wood River, IL: Ron Snyder & Associates, 1985.

Stevenson, Katherine Cole, and H. Ward Jandl. *Houses by Mail: A Guide to Houses from Sears, Roebuck and Company*. New York: Preservation Press, 1986.

Time Life Books. *This Fabulous Century, 1900–1910*. NJ: Time, Inc., 1969.

Weil, Gordon L. *Sears, Roebuck, U.S.A. The Great American Catalog Store and How It Grew*. New York: Stein and Day Publishers, 1977.

Worthy, James C. *Shaping an American Institution; Robert E. Wood and Sears, Roebuck*. Chicago: University of Illinois, 1984.

MAGAZINES

American Builder (note: *American Carpenter and Builder* was renamed *American Builder* in 1917). "Cypress: The Wood Eternal" (advertisement), March 1920, 21.
———. "Electric Handsaw Cuts Costs," February 1925, 236.
———. "Home Ownership Means Security," June 1920, 73.
———. "How the Contractor Can Help Finance Home Building," June 1919, 73.
———. "Miracle City (Wood River) Builds Modern High School," December 1920, 120.
———. "Reducing the Cost of the Workman's House," December 1917, 40.

American Carpenter and Builder Magazine, Chicago, IL. Advertisement for Sears and Roebuck, February 1911, 111.
———. Advertisement for Sears and Roebuck, February 1912.
———. Advertisement for Sears and Roebuck, June 1910, 95.
———. Advertisement for Sears and Roebuck, June 1912, 119.
———. Advertisement for Sears and Roebuck, March 1912.
———. "Bungalows Only: A Novel Building Restriction at Gary, Indiana," May 1915, 40.
———. "Dealers and Contractors Need Good House Plan Service," December 1916, 42.

Business Week, New York. "Mail Order House Links Up Realtors," April 23, 1930, p. 16.
———. "New Installment Plan for Home Building," January 29, 1930, p. 10.
———. "Quantity Production Reaches the Homebuilder," March 26, 1930, p. 25.
———. "Sears and Housing," September 2, 1939, pp. 27-28.
———. "Two Mail Order Houses Now Are Building Homes," March 5, 1930, p. 17.

Fortune, New York. "The Catalogue as Historian," February 1932, 132.
———. "The Great American Salesman," February 1932, 124.
———. "Mass-produced Houses in Review," April 1933, 52–58.

Stanolind Record, Whiting, IN. "Brief Review of the Growth of Wood River Refinery," October 1919, 30.
———. "Enter Standard Oil, and It's Different," December 1919, 14
———. "Carlinville," August 1925, 40.
———. "Carlinville," July 1925, 41.
———. "Carlinville," June 1925, 46.
———. "Carlinville," October 1921, 49.
———. "Carlinville," September 1921, 53.
———. "Carlinville/Schoper," March 21, 1921, 49.
———. "Model Mine and Miners' Homes at Carlinville, Illinois," December 1919, 17.
———. "Standard Addition, Carlinville, Illinois," September 1923, 19–21.
———. "Standard Oil (Indiana) and the Community," August 1921, 36.

Newspapers

Cairo Citizen, Cairo, IL. "Building Switch at Sears and Roebuck Plant," July 8, 1911.
———. "Cairo Given Another Boost," March 14, 1912
———. "Half a Million to Be Cost of New Sears and Roebuck Plant," July 29, 1911.
———. "Over 100 Autos in Cairo," March 25, 1911.
———. "Property of Lumber Plant Is Sold Here," December 10, 1955.
———. "Sears and Roebuck Bought 30-Acre Tract in North Cairo," May 26, 1911.
———. "Sears and Roebuck Closed Deal for Site," May 19, 1911.
———. "Sears and Roebuck Officials in Cairo," July 28, 1911.
———. "Sears and Roebuck to Get $3,500 Bonus to Locate Here," May 23, 1911.

Chicago Tribune. "Looking Ahead with Business: Sears Roebuck," January 22, 1931.
———. "Sears Roebuck Addition; $250,000 Plant to Be Built at Cairo," May 21, 1911.
———. "Some Illinois Coal Miners' Homes and a Typical Family," November 3, 1919.

New York Times. "Sees Future Homes Bought Like Autos," May 25, 1932

Wall Street Journal. "Sears Will Expand Home Construction," January 22, 1932, 5.

Catalogs

1908–1940 Sears Modern Homes Catalogs
1908 General Merchandise Catalog
1912 Successful Building Book (promotional booklet for Sears Homes)
1914 Building Materials Catalog
1931 Summer Cottages
1933 (approximate date) Garages, Lob Cabins, Playhouses, Cottages Catalog
1935 Honor Bilt Building Materials Catalog
1948 and 1951 Homart Homes Catalogs

Honor Bilt Homes (Sears Roebuck and Company) Brochures

Cypress, The Wood Eternal. N.d.
Honor Bilt Homes Make Happy Homes. N.d.

Websites

www.kithouse.org
www.searshomes.org
www.wardwayhomes.com

About the Author

Rose Thornton is the author of several books, including *The Houses That Sears Built* (2002), *Finding the Houses That Sears Built* (2004) and *The Ugly Woman's Guide to Internet Dating* (2009). She's the coauthor of *California's Kit Homes* (2004) and *Montgomery Wards Mail-Order Homes* (2010).

Rose has traveled to twenty-four states to give two hundred lectures on Sears homes, from Bungalow Heaven in Los Angeles to the Smithsonian in Washington, D.C. She has addressed a wide variety of audiences from architectural preservationists in Boston, St. Louis and Chicago to kit home enthusiasts in small towns across America.

Rose has appeared on MSNBC, PBS (*History Detectives*), A&E (*Biography*) and CBS (*Sunday Morning News*), and her book was featured in its own category on *Jeopardy!*. She is considered the country's number-one authority on kit homes. Her work has been featured in the *Wall Street Journal*, *New York Times*, *Christian Science Monitor*, *Washington Post*, *L.A. Times*, *Dallas Morning News*, *Old House Journal*, *American Bungalow*, *Blue Ridge Country* and about one hundred other publications. Twice in the last five years, the story of her unique career was picked up by the AP, and in May 2009, she was interviewed on BBC Radio.